The Guidebook to
ESP and
Psychic Wonders

The Guidebook to
ESP and
Psychic Wonders

Katherine Fair Donnelly

David McKay Company, Inc.

NEW YORK

Library of Congress Cataloging in Publication Data

Donnelly, Katherine Fair.
  The guidebook to ESP and psychic wonders.

  Bibliography: p.
  Includes index.
  1. Psychical research. I. Title.
BF1031.D66   133.8   77–15802
ISBN 0–679–50805–8

10 9 8 7 6 5 4 3 2 1

Manufactured in the United States of America

Dedicated to:

JOHN H. DONNELLY
  . . . for the Guiding Light he is . . .

LAWRENCE LESHAN
  . . . for the Guiding Light he was . . .

EILEEN J. GARRETT—In Memoriam
  . . . for the Guiding Light she always will be

Contents

PART IV

Acknowledgments

I should like to express my deep gratitude to:

- Rose Fair, my very special mother, and to Fannie and Sam Arkind, Zetta and Jerry Fair, and Trudy and Alex Zomper for their abiding faith.

- Vera R. Webster, who was the catalyst responsible for making this possible, and whose kindnesses and courtesies are unending.

- Betty J. Kelly, who bombarded me with books on psychic matters, which literally formed the home library for much of my research.

- Paul Beard and Ruby Yeatman, who were bricks from the onset, and who tirelessly answered my inquiries.

- Hugh G. Henkel for his fine hand and guidance in the vastly complex area of permissions.

- Ruth Hannon, without whose encouragement this book would not have been written.

- Joanne Michaels, Sydne Silverstein, Barbara Machtiger and Rainelle Peters for their many helpful suggestions.

- and, most of all, to John H. Donnelly, for his encouragement and support, without which this book most certainly could not have been written.

I am particularly grateful to those individuals who were kind enough to hear or read this manuscript in its various stages and to permit me their comments and reactions: Eileen Coly, Lynn Hunsucker, Eda LeShan, Dr. Lawrence LeShan, Andrea Fodor Litkei, Edith Marshall, Orin Marshall, Dr. T. Nyilas, John L. Travis, and Ruby Yeatman.

It is my pleasure to thank the American Society for Psychical Research staff members—Laura F. Knipe and Marian Nester—for their fine assistance in very many ways. I should also like to express my thanks to the staff of the Parapsychology Foundation for their help: Alan Angoff, Grazina Babusis, Lisette Coly, Lesley Poole, and Betty Shapin.

A most special thank-you to Medelicia Delgado for permitting me to borrow her electric typewriter.

Responsibility for inadequacies, of course, rests solely with the author.

K.F.D.

Preface

This is a story about me—and about you, your family, your friends, and your neighbors.

Perhaps your story will not happen in exactly the same way as mine, but it will be similar. This is a book about experiences I had, which I later learned were psychic in nature and fell into the realm of ESP. It is also a book about questions I had after I learned the nature of these experiences. Since I did not know the answers, I sought them from those who did. I then wanted to share with others the benefits of answers from experts in the psychic field. That is why this book was written, so that the views of knowledgeable individuals—ones highly respected in their field—could be expressed to those seeking explanations as I did.

TO THE SKEPTICS AMONG US:

There is a principle which is a bar against all information, which is proof against all arguments, which cannot fail to keep a man in everlasting ignorance; that principle is contempt, prior to investigation.

—Herbert Spencer

PART I

CHAPTER

1

The Beginning

The Awakening/Psychic Phenomena

It was the month of October and the day after my operation for cancer. I was thirty-five.

I regained consciousness in the quiet and softly lit room in Harkness Pavilion of Columbia Presbyterian Hospital, dimly aware of a figure cloaked in white at my bedside.

Drifting back into a semisleep, the wonderment of it all enveloped me, whisking my thoughts back in time, back to the many months before the operation.

I was remembering some of the incredible events that ultimately led me into this hushed hospital room, remembering one special morning after a curious dream. At the breakfast table, I had told my husband about it: "I dreamed I went to see our family doctor, and after examining me, he turned to me and said, 'If you were my wife, I would send you to see Dr. John Conley.' "

I had never heard of a Dr. John Conley. But, why did I dream of his name?

My husband suggested that I see our family doctor as soon as possible, which I did a few days later, but told him nothing of my dream. I had asked my husband to accompany me for this visit, as a sense of uneasiness seemed wrapped around me. After his examination, the doctor turned to me and said, "If you were my wife, I would send you to see Dr. John Conley."

What mysterious force had entered my mind during the sleeping stage when I dreamed—days in advance—what my doctor would say to me? It was surely a frightening experience for someone unknowledgeable of psychic phenomena.

After I had seen the distinguished Dr. John Conley and a team of doctors, a biopsy was performed. It was determined I had cancer. Dr. Robin Rankow, Chief Surgeon of Columbia Presbyterian Hospital, a truly gifted man, performed the surgery, for which I shall ever be grateful. On each of the birthdays I have celebrated since, I have written to this magnificent man to thank him for helping make them possible.

The questions I posed to myself after that surgery, and the questions still posed today are: What would have happened if I had *not* had the dream about the visit to my doctor's office? Would I have gone to see a doctor at that point in time? Had this been so important a dream that it had actually saved my life?

When speaking with the doctor after the surgery, my husband was told that had we waited six weeks longer, it might have been too late.

And so, we arrive at the real story in this book—not the story of me, or my operation for whatever problem—but the story of *why* I had such a dream, *when* I did, and an attempt to provide to others who have had similar mysterious experiences explanations from those who are expert in the matters of such psychic phenomena.

Bless Mrs. Robinson/Synchronicity

When I learned that I was to be operated on for cancer, I immediately wanted to put my house in order—in every way. I calmly made funeral arrangements, not wishing to be dramatic, but wishing to envisage any eventuality. I then set about literally putting my house in order.

I telephoned an agency that provided cleaning help for households and was absolutely delighted when I learned the name of my helper was to be "Mrs. Robinson." For some unaccountable reason, for which I have no satisfactory explanation to date, the name Robinson has always meant something special to me, always favorable, and I took it as an especially good omen that God, in this very trying time in my life, chose to send me a helper bearing that name.

But by the next morning I was highly nervous. Mrs. Robinson was due to report that day at 9:00 A.M. At 8:00 A.M., I put on my coat and left the house, walking toward the subway station. I stood rooted at the entrance for almost twenty minutes. A group of people were coming up the stairs, out to where I was standing on the street. Just behind them was a woman dressed neatly in a black overcoat. There was nothing to distinguish this woman from the rest of the people, yet I felt moved to speak to her.

"Pardon me," I inquired, "but are you Mrs. Robinson?"

"No," she answered. I explained that I was expecting a helper from the agency and did not want her to get lost. The woman then told me that she was the cleaning helper from the agency and that Mrs. Robinson was unable to come.

"Oh," I exclaimed, "and what is your name?"

She looked at me and slowly replied, "I am Mrs. Graves."

As soon as I heard the name "Graves," my heart sank. The buoyancy and joy I had felt the day before when hearing the name Robinson now deserted me completely, leaving in their place fear and despair. The gravity of the operation suddenly struck me with full force. Was I indeed going to my grave? What had happened to Mrs. Robinson? Why had God so deserted me?

A week later, struggling to consciousness in the hushed hospital room, I turned my head toward the figure in white at my bedside. "You're a strange one," the kindly nurse chided me. "Usually upon awakening, a patient asks for a mother, a husband, a father . . . but you asked me what my name was."

Peering up at the cloudy mist of white, I whispered, "What is your name?"

"Mrs. Robinson," the nurse replied.

God *was* on my side after all. What I, as a novice, didn't know was that in His vocabulary of psychic miracles there is a definition for Mrs. Robinson.

It is called "synchronicity."

The Easter Sunday Vision/ESP

For some months prior to my operation in October, mysterious occurrences kept happening to me—events so unusual they simply could not be explained in ordinary terms. Like most people, I had heard of ESP, but knew relatively little about it.

On Easter Sunday of that year, I had an extraordinary experience. I "saw" a "vision!" We had been visiting in Wilmington, Delaware, and were en route to New York by train. As we approached Grand Central Station, my husband began to shake my arm, "Wake up, we're almost there."

"I'm not asleep," I replied. Although I hadn't been sleeping, I seemed to be in a state of semiawakeness, and had just "seen" a vision in the mud-spattered window of the train.

I was stunned! I had never seen a vision before. This had simply come out of the blue—a moving picture of events which appeared before me on the windowpane, much as a movie would on a screen. What I "saw" was this:

At Grand Central Station, we took a taxi. The taxi driver announced he would take a short cut. During the ride, I turned anxiously to my husband and told him that when we arrived home, there would be a mouse in our foyer, but that the mouse would be half dead and half alive, that upon entering the house my husband would stamp his foot, but that the mouse wouldn't run, just wiggle its tail.

As our train pulled slowly into Grand Central Station, I related the vision to my husband. I had clearly seen the events depicted, but did not know why.

During our taxi ride home, the driver announced he knew a short cut— just as he had in the vision. I anxiously turned to my husband and told him of my dismay, that I *knew* there would be a mouse in our foyer half dead and half alive. My husband tried to calm my fears, but upon our arrival home, my apprehensions grew. When the door to our foyer was opened, there lay the mouse. My husband stamped his foot, but the mouse did not move . . . just wiggled its tail.

A feeling of uneasiness crept around me and, for some unaccountable reason, I felt that little mouse was a portent of things to come with regard to my own well-being—and that while I did not feel sick, there was something very much wrong with my health.

One thing I did know: Whatever it was that had caused me to be able to "see" this vision, it was something I had never experienced before.

What I did not know then was that I was destined soon to meet one of the world's most famous mediums—who would not only offer explanations for these strange new experiences but would also perform *psychic healing* on me at a crucial time in my life—a healer who had helped in cancer research, experimenting in healing some of God's smaller creatures: Mice!

Garrote and Mrs. Garrett/Psychic Healing

During the year before I entered the hospital, I had one particular dream several times—one in which I was being garroted about the neck.

Webster's definition of garrote states it is a ". . . mode of execution by strangulation with an iron collar. . . ." But why was I having dreams of garroting?

One morning, I was obsessed suddenly with the idea that I must go downstairs to the lobby of our building at once. I quickly grabbed a robe, threw it on, and ran to the elevator. As the door opened into the lobby, I didn't have any idea why I was there . . . I simply stood transfixed for a time. Some moments later, a woman with electrifying eyes appeared, swathed in a fur hat and fur coat. I did not know her, yet some inexplicable force moved me to address her. I was astonished to hear my voice call out a name. "Mrs. Garrett?" I asked.

"Yes," she replied. "Do I know you?"

"No," I answered. She smiled and we said goodbye.

As I rode upstairs in the elevator, I thought to myself how curious it was that I had a dream about "garrote" and that I had met a Mrs. "Garrett" in such a strange way—almost as if I were being warned of something.

Months later—after the surgery had been performed—we learned that the lymph nodes and glands that were removed had formed a rope effect around my neck—like a garrote!

But who was Mrs. Garrett, and what was she doing in the lobby of our apartment house? I later learned that we shared the same family doctor, whose offices adjoined that lobby.

Following the operation, there were still more strange occurrences. I went to see our family physician, Dr. Tibor Nyilas, and told him of some of the events taking place. He suggested I see a Mrs. Eileen J. Garrett who was president of the Parapsychology Foundation in New York, and a world-famous medium—the same Mrs. Garrett I had met in the lobby.

On my first visit with Eileen Garrett, we quickly formed a unique and warm relationship, the memory of which I shall always treasure. Later, Eileen performed psychic healing on me, at a time when I felt myself slipping very badly physically, almost a sinking type of feeling—as if I were not quite going to make it after all—and we both sensed it was a crucial time in my life. After the psychic healing, I still felt very weak and sapped of strength.

Shortly thereafter, however, I started to show signs of definite improvement. I began to feel alive and vibrant. It was in this period that I learned how heavily engaged Eileen Garrett had been in cancer research with mice.

Eileen introduced me to Dr. Lawrence LeShan, a highly respected parapsychologist and well-known author, at that time working with Eileen at the Parapsychology Foundation, as well as being affiliated with the Union Theological Seminary. I later was to learn that he, too, had been deeply committed to helping cancer patients in hospitals. It was Dr. LeShan who would one day suggest I visit the College of Psychic Sciences in London, where I would learn answers to many of my questions.

Lawrence LeShan devoted countless hours of his time and energies to helping me. I once asked him how I could hope to repay his kindness to me. "Just pass it along," he replied.

And so, to "pass it along" is the real purpose of this book.

The Trail Begins

Clairvoyance . . . apports . . . psychometry . . . psychokinesis . . . precognition . . . ghosts and spirits . . . sensitives . . . dowsing . . . automatic writing . . . mediums . . . controls . . . premonitions . . . telepathy . . . out of body . . . reincarnation . . . retrocognition . . . psi . . . psychic healing . . . poltergeists . . . extrasensory perception . . . auras . . .

How technical so many of the terms sounded to me! As I began to seek explanations for the events I had been experiencing, I was not necessarily looking for abbreviated explanations but, I hoped, some that were uncomplicated and simple enough for me to be comfortable with—some that I could relate to easily. I wanted to know what these experiences were called. I wanted to understand how they might differ from or be the same as the experiences of my friends, neighbors, relatives.

Although I sought answers and explanations to my own experiences, I would shy away from reading what appeared to be "deep" or "heavy" material. While I wanted to know and understand some so-called "psychic" terms, at the same time I was extremely apprehensive. I was reluctant to venture too far lest I drown—with no handy lifesaver available.

The search for explanations led me to many doors, both in America and in England. As each door opened, I was overwhelmed by the seemingly "too-complex-for-me" findings. So many of the long and scientific-sounding words frightened me and I would quickly turn away from them. I was able to accept some of the ideas and theories, but I kept coming across what I call "five-dollar" words, as opposed to those, say, for twenty-five cents, the latter being far easier for a layman to understand.

The views of a number of experts in psychic studies are expressed in the pages of this book. In all fairness, opinions contrary to those views are also stated, as well as those of researchers sophisticated in the psychoanalytical area. As will be pointed out later, the latter group maintains that most psychic experiences are merely expressions of the unconscious mind and not ESP.

It is my earnest hope that much of this material is presented in the "twenty-five-cent-and-up" range, and that the reader will not be afraid of some of the more intricate phrases in the upper range. There will be some instances when the writer could not hope to compete with the manner in which a phrase is turned by many of these experts. For this reason, rather than attempting to paraphrase into what might be "twenty-five-cent" words, I have chosen to quote in specific areas. The experts not only say it far better than I could, but it is important that you learn from the wisdom of their knowledge.

If you feel you cannot comprehend some areas, put the book aside for a while, and come back to it. If there are questions you still have, write to me in care of my publisher, and I will try my best to unravel the problem. I am a layman just like you. I sought explanations to psychic experiences, and I was lucky—very lucky. I, by the grace of God, was led to most of the fine people I have met in this field, and I would like to share the benefits of their guidance and help. And because I truly believe it is the mind that makes the body rich, I also want to share with you quotations from many of the books, which might not be easily accessible.

In order to provide a cross segment on many psychic matters, it would have been unfair of me to limit the material to works related to my own experiences. It is my earnest hope that in presenting these ABCs of ESP that I have at least met the qualifying standards of attempting to explain some of the many unique and diverse views and terms of this expanding field.

I will not go into a long description here of all of the individuals and organizations appearing in this book. These will appear in the related chapters to provide insight as to who these experts are. However, you will be hearing a great deal about the College of Psychic Studies in London, the American Society for Psychical Research, and the Parapsychology Foundation in New York. So, it is important at this point to establish the credentials of the individuals associated with these organizations.

Paul Beard is currently the president of the College of Psychic Studies, and has been highly respected in the field of psychic phenomena for more than forty years. He is the author of *Survival of Death* and has given over seventy lectures in the last few years, including those to the Society for Psychical Research. Mr. Beard is admirably qualified, and the reader will have the benefit of his answers to questions asked of him in various sections of this book.

Ruby Yeatman, former secretary, librarian, and principal of the College of Psychic Studies (formerly known as the College of Psychic Sciences), has spent almost thirty-five years there meeting and greeting the "great" minds in the field of psychic sciences. She was responsible for interviewing all those who came to the College in need of help, as well as supervising arrangements for sittings with mediums. She is eminently qualified, and to talk with Ruby Yeatman is to spend an illuminating hour indeed. In addition to answering a number of complex questions about psychic phenomena during the preparation of this book, Miss Yeatman also supplied a major part of the selected Bibliography and the Additional Reading Selections, which are included at the end.

I feel uniquely and singularly honored that both Paul Beard and Ruby Yeatman permitted me to pass along to you their answers to my many questions regarding psychic matters.

The College of Psychic Studies itself was founded in 1884 to further inquiry into psychical and allied psychological fields. There is a library of over 10,000 volumes. Weekly lectures are held through most of the year, as well as weekend workshops, classes for meditation, and many brief lecture courses given by distinguished personalities in the psychic field. The College operates a system of distant psychic healing, which enables healers to work in their own homes. A quarterly journal, entitled *Light*, is sponsored by the College and contains articles by well-known writers on aspects of psychical research and evidence for survival of bodily death and on the inner nature of man. It has a worldwide circulation. The College also maintains a small fund to assist a limited number of members and visitors who desire sittings with sensitives but who cannot afford to pay the normal fee.

The American Society for Psychical Research is a nonprofit organization that provides the public with a great deal of basic information on psychic subjects. Its purpose is to advance the understanding of phenomena thought to be paranormal: telepathy, clairvoyance, precognition, psychokinesis, and related occurrences that at present are not explicable in terms of physical, psychological, and biological theories.

This prestigious organization was founded in 1885, with Simon Newcomb, the well-known astronomer, as its president, and in later years, was under the guidance of the distinguished psychologist, William James, and James Hyslop, formerly professor of logic and ethics at Columbia University. Currently, the renowned and highly respected Dr. Montague Ullman is president. Formerly head of the Department of Psychiatry at Maimonides Medical Center, Dr. Ullman is noted for his fine work in the parapsychological field and his writings on dream studies in telepathy.

Aiding the public in their quest for understanding psychic phenomena is the very important and difficult task of Mrs. Laura F. Knipe, Executive Secretary of the ASPR. If the Society does not have the information needed, Mrs. Knipe provides help as to where details can be obtained. She also meets with visitors who have questions regarding psychic matters, the ASPR library, or membership.

Research in ESP with psychics and sensitives is currently being conducted at the ASPR by the distinguished Dr. Karlis Osis, research fellow and psychologist. At the present time, he is working in research on life after death, directing laboratory experimentation on out-of-body experiences.

One of the leading authorities in the psychic field is Mrs. Laura A. Dale, editor of the *ASPR Journal*, who has been with the society for over twenty-five years and has done a great deal in experimental work.

The *ASPR Newsletter* consists of short reports on research, education, and various activities in parapsychology. The newest paperbound publication of the ASPR is *Exploring ESP and PK*, a collation of twenty-seven key articles from the *Newsletter*, written by top professionals in the field in "lay language." Students, teachers, discussion leaders, and interested lay-people who want to know of current developments in the psychic field will find this most useful. *Exploring ESP and PK* may be obtained at a nominal charge by writing to the ASPR at 5 West 73 Street, New York, New York 10023. (Additional information on publications can be found in the appendix of this book.)

Should the reader wish information on the 16-page directory of educational courses at universities in your area that offer lectures and instruction, send your inquiry to Mrs. Marian Nester, Education Department, at the above address, together with a stamped, self-addressed envelope.

This book could not have been written without the help of Mrs. Eileen Coly, president of the Parapsychology Foundation in New York. Mrs. Coly brings to the Foundation her unique capabilities as an administrator and guides it with a firm hand. She also has the unique insight that being the daughter of Eileen Garrett could provide.

The Parapsychology Foundation was established in 1951 by Eileen J. Garrett, the renowned psychic researcher, author, and medium. Its goals, said Mrs. Coly, quoting from Eileen Garrett's writing, were, and still are, to find "resources that could provide grants to those who sought after a wider horizon in reading. . . . This would involve a library . . . to answer the demands for literature and eventual study for those who might be ready to work in a parapsychological atmosphere. Finally . . . to bring scholars together from different countries for discussion, as well as . . . to keep contacts alive if eventual advancement of the theoretical discussion were to result in action."

Since Eileen Garrett's death in 1970, Mrs. Coly and her colleagues at the foundation have carried on in the tradition of Mrs. Garrett, "seeking always the goals she set, searching for an understanding of the laws and principles which underlie paranormal human behavior, encouraging the varied approaches to the scientific quest for a better understanding of the psychic elements in our world."

There are some in the field of parapsychology who do not feel that the layperson should delve into the psychic area. Further, it is believed by some in the medical profession as well as others that overly sensitive people who think they have had psychic experiences should first consult with a psychologist with an understanding of parapsychology before probing deeply into this subject.

While this may be a perfectly valid recommendation and solution for some individuals seeking guidance in the psychic field, it would seem hardly fair to limit knowledge of psychic matters to a scientific elite—just as, if a small percentage of the population were allergic to the wheat in bread, it would hardly seem fair that the entire populace be asked not to partake of it.

Those individuals who feel they have had and continue to have psychic experiences do have other alternatives and may wish to contact groups interested in psychic matters. Information on these organizations, as well as information on psychic magazines, books (and where to find books not easily obtainable), tapes, journals, and newsletters, may be found listed in the Selected Bibliography and Appendix of this book.

No matter how I attempt to present ESP and its psychic "relatives," I am bound to receive criticism from varying quarters. However, if just one of the chapters in this book enlightens you as to the nature of ESP, this book will have served its purpose.

3

What Is Psychic Healing?

What does it feel like to receive psychic healing? Who performs it? Where is it done? What other types of healing are there, and how are they performed? Is "laying on of hands" considered part of psychic healing?

These are only some of the questions people have asked. In my own experience, I was singularly blessed and had the extraordinary good fortune to have had psychic healing performed on me by one of the greatest mediums in the world—Eileen J. Garrett.

Eileen Garrett was many women—clairvoyant, author, psychic researcher, lecturer, and healer, as well as being the president of the Parapsychology Foundation. Of all her talents—which included telepathy, precognition, clairaudience, trance mediumship, and many others—she most highly valued her ability to function as a healer and to diagnose and analyze illness through clairvoyant perception. She worked in conjunction with physicians, psychologists, and others in the medical profession in helping with the recovery or maintenance of the well-being of others.

After an operation for cancer I felt completely drained of strength. I was so weak I could barely hold my head erect. I remember sitting in a chair. Eileen stood in back of me, placed her hands on either side of my head, and then she put them on my neck and shoulder. She then began to speak to the blood and asked that the blood be directed properly in its flow. Eileen asked a member of her staff to be present in order to observe the coloration of my knees. Eileen continued speaking to the blood, after which she inquired if the color had turned red. I heard the reply, "Yes, the knees are quite red now."

The healing itself did not take very long by the clock, but to me it seemed a marvelously long time, at the end of which I felt serene and relaxed. I felt an inexplicable comfort. There was no feeling, however, of special relief or extra energy. I did not feel this until many weeks later, at which time I began to feel vibrant again. I experienced a feeling of "being alive," whereas before I felt as if I was slipping at a rapid pace into a perilous decline. I "knew" that Eileen was literally acting as a lifesaver, and that I had been drowning. The need for psychic healing in no way detracted from the superb surgery performed. As I reflect upon it, the healing was an adjunct to the surgery much as a pair of crutches would serve as an aid to a person with a broken leg in a cast.

Of the many books Eileen wrote, one in particular deals with her personal philosophy on healing: *Life Is the Healer*. I feel this book should be regarded as a landmark in the concept of psychic healing. If you read no other book on healing in your lifetime, I urge you to locate a copy. I quote from it Eileen's advice on choosing a legitimate healer:

"For it is supremely important to everyone who is or may be in need of healing, not to fall into the hands of quacks, fakers or charlatans. How can we know whether a healer . . . is worthy of trust?

"There are, it seems to me, three ways of testing. . . . The first test of the validity of a healer, therefore, is his own sincere vocation *as* a healer, including his willingness without reservation to enter into a close, human relationship with the patient. . . .

"Is he sincere? Does he have a genuine, recognizable desire to help those in distress? Or is his attitude mainly commercial? (This test applied to any healer whether 'unorthodox' or 'orthodox.' The physician who may have graduated from the best medical schools but who is primarily interested in money rather than in healing is in my estimation simply a money-maker whose business happens to be medicine. He has no *vocation* for the healing arts, and by numbering himself among those who do he is engaging in false representation for the sake of gain. Such a person, no matter what his background or lack of it, whether 'orthodox' or 'unorthodox' is no true healer and should be trusted by nobody.) . . . There are sound reasons for testing first of all the genuineness of the healer's vocation to be a healer. . . . The day is past, or rapidly passing, when anyone claiming to be in any respect a healer can operate by considering the patient as simply another mechanism to be repaired.

"The second test we can all apply is this: Does the professed healer himself understand and work with the forces that make for life? . . . The third test of professed healers, whether 'unorthodox' or not, is of course the pragmatic test: Does what he does, *work?* Does he heal? For there is no argument against clear evidence."[1]

Cautioning against professed healers who make extravagant claims, Eileen advises us to listen to what a healer has to say and to estimate him by it:

"If, for example, he asserts that he can heal because he is the seventh son of a seventh son, or because he was born with a caul, or because he is of royal descent, one is safe in deciding to look elsewhere. If, on the other hand, the healer shows understanding of the curative power of life itself, together with a deep desire joined with some ability to help the patient benefit from the power that makes for wholeness, it may matter little whether he knows human anatomy or what functions various organs perform."[2]

1. Garrett, *Life Is the Healer*, pp. 79, 80, 81.
2. Ibid., p. 81.

Eileen advises that when exercising some skepticism, and in evaluating the genuineness of healers, it is equally important to keep an open mind—and not challenge or disbelieve that a thing is actually true with the idea that such things cannot and do not happen. A harsh foe of truth is unwillingness to accept evidence previously thought of as inconceivable: "Jesus summed it all up when He said: 'None are so blind as those who *will not* see.' "3

Mrs. Garrett speaks of the incredible history of paths men chart for themselves even when confronted with clear evidence of healing:

"Nobody in his right mind will dispute this in theory—yet it is a strange phenomenon of history that men often *choose* to disbelieve in what is before their eyes incontrovertibly. Usually, they refuse to meet the issue of fact head on, but attempt to discredit the healer on other grounds which they fondly but illogically assume will somehow erase the healing fact"4

Eileen had been often asked by people of many faiths if the philosophy of healing she espoused was a substitute for religious faith:

"I am often asked by sincere and intelligent people: 'Is there conflict between my religious faith . . . and "unorthodox healing" as you understand and teach it?'

"In all cases . . . the only reply I can give is an emphatic 'No!' There is no conflict between spiritually based healing and any of the historic forms of the Christian faith, or with the teachings of those whose religion is derived from . . . the 'Old Testament.' On the contrary, all the faiths mentioned (and others as well) have for many, many centuries taught the reality of spiritual healing and have in varying degrees made its practice a part of their life. What possibly could be heterodox about the belief that the God who made the universe can heal His afflicted children—especially when His prophets and disciples have declared that this is so, over and over? In fact it is something of an irony that what we call 'unorthodox' healing has from the beginning been deeply imbedded in the spiritual heritage of unquestionably *orthodox* religion."5

I remember a conversation with Eileen shortly after one of many operations I had undergone within a period of several years. Indulging myself in the warmth of Eileen's protective wing and angry with events, I exclaimed, "Well, I absolutely refuse to undergo any more surgery." Eileen was walking toward a window and upon hearing my words turned full around to me and emphatically stated: "*You* will *do* exactly as your doctors *say* you must do!" It was supremely important to Eileen that the body and the mind be attuned in all ways, and she took pride in being able to work with the medical profession in achieving these goals.

Dr. Lawrence LeShan, the noted author and parapsychologist, describes the different types of healers and to what they attribute their abilities:

"The largest group of healers described their work as 'prayer' and believed their success was due to the intervention of God. A second group

3. Ibid., p. 81.
4. Ibid., pp. 81, 82.
5. Ibid., p. 105.

believed the healing was done by 'Spirits' after they had set up a special linkage between the spirits and the patient and the third group believed that they were transmitters or originators of some special form of 'energy' that had healing effects."[6]

Because I had so very many questions on this subject, I wrote to Paul Beard, the president of the College of Psychic Studies in England. I had met Paul in London, and whenever I spoke with him, I always came away feeling enlightened. I felt it would be a marvelous boon to others like myself if he would provide some insight into the area of psychic healing. Here are some of his astute observations and explanations:

What is psychic healing? Why is it called "psychic" healing? "So-called psychic healing can be of several kinds. First there is magnetic healing where the healer possesses an abundance of magnetic near-physical energy which he imparts to the patient, thereby giving the patient a boost of energy which may enable his body to resume its proper health pattern.

"Next there is healing which is directed primarily to the relieving of symptoms. When this is successful, again the patient receives the opportunity for his body to re-establish its normal health patterns. A danger exists however when symptom relieving is made the main purpose of the healing because symptoms are part of the body's language of warning and information giving. Symptoms are for a trained doctor to interpret. If symptoms are relieved without such interpretation then the 'healing' may do little more than mask nature's wise advice and perhaps give the patient a false confidence so that he does not realize that his symptoms may have been pointing to a deep-seated illness requiring extended medical or hospital treatment.

"Next we have treatment which is directed towards the emotional and mental vehicles of the patient. It is here where a very great deal of disease, or dis-ease, resides. Symptoms and illnesses can well be the result of such mental and emotional imbalance or stress. The purpose of healing of this kind is to put the patient into touch with his own wiser interior self, of which his daily self may be almost completely ignorant and also to put him in touch with the forces of harmony and wisdom which spring from the beneficent forces at the heart of the universe, whether such forces are looked upon as produced by a personal God or an impersonal force. In such a type of healing relaxation on the part of the patient is an important factor for this is an aid in allowing his own hidden wisdom gradually to impart itself to his consciousness. For this reason patients receiving this type of healing very often start by reporting no change in their physical condition but a very marked change in their attitude, both towards their illness and toward their life-pattern and toward the world in general. This is the type of healing which is carried out at the College of Psychic Studies.

"Next there is a type of healing which is primarily directed to the re-alignment and adjustment of long-seated physical defects such as defective eye-sight, mis-alignments of the spine, arthritis and other illnesses, many

6. LeShan, *The Medium, the Mystic and the Physicist*, pp. 102–3.

of which have the characteristic of imposing a degree of immobility of some kind or another upon the patient. This type of healing is usually carried out by the virtuoso type of healer, such as Harry Edwards. Harry Edwards declares that the healing power is very swift and he is often able to perform instant and remarkable changes, many of which release the immobility from which the patient has suffered. The patient can then get up, walk about, touch his toes, and perform movements he could not have done before the treatment started. The effects of such treatment may be long-lasting, or they may be comparatively brief. This depends upon the inner attitude of the patient. It is not every patient who is really willing to be cured, or who can accept the consequences of restoration to a fuller life than he or she may have enjoyed for a number of years past.

"Lastly, there is spiritual healing proper. It is very difficult to speak of this or to be aware when it is operating. It arises by nature of what a theologian will call Grace. From an outer aspect it might almost seem as if a patient is being given a new opportunity to live a normal life. Such a healing might then be an event which the patient has spiritually earned. Orthodox Christian and other religious healers tend to look for this type of healing and to accept that it comes about through a charismatic gift on the part of the healers. In my view it is usually the patient who by a helpful interior attitude has earned the right to the healing, rather than the healer having some special priestly, sacramental power at his command. Not everyone, however, will agree to this sort of statement.

"The term 'psychic healing' is a vague one and does not distinguish much of the processes which may be involved in various sorts of healing."

We look now to Dr. LeShan for some insight as to who might be considered psychic healers:

"I assembled a list of individuals who could be described as serious psychic healers. These included all the individuals whom I felt reasonably certain *did* accomplish results in this area, who worked consistently in it, and about whom there was either autobiographical or good biographical material. It consisted primarily of Olga and Ambrose Worrall, Harry Edwards, Rebecca Beard, Agnes Sanford, Edgar Jackson, the Christian Science group, Paramahansa Yogananda, Stewart Grayson, and Katherine Kuhlmann. A variety of other healers, ranging from Padre Pio to Mrs. Salmon and Sai Baba, were also studied in this way through the material which was available on them."[7]

In the following chapter you will read a great deal about Ambrose and Olga Worrall, two extremely dedicated, devout, and sincere healers. You will also learn about their work at the New Life Clinic in Baltimore. Let us now, however, turn to another one of the healers mentioned both by Paul Beard and Dr. LeShan. Harry Edwards clarifies how healings obtained wide acceptance:

"Those people who, for some reason or another, discount the reality of spiritual healing and say that the healings arose from self-hypnosis and

7. Ibid., pp. 104–5.

suggestion, the exercise of will power, or that those so helped are all neurotics and hypochondriacs, have to face the cold logic that the healing movement could not have earned such wide acceptance unless the healings were factual; its growth could not have been dependent upon the testimony of people who were unsound in their outlooks. They are faced with a mass of evidence which shows that many who were diagnosed to be gravely ill from incurable conditions, for which medical science could do no more, have made complete recoveries without any further trace of symptoms of their diseases.

"In my personal experience, healers have been privileged to deal with successful people in all walks of life, including the Royal Family, judges, politicians, war commanders, generals, admirals, doctors and theologians, celebrities in the entertainment world and so on, right through the strata of society. Surely all these people are not fools or self-deluded neurotics?"[8]

Donald Galloway, well-known sensitive and author, tells of a time when he collapsed at business. After being rushed home, a doctor was summoned and Don was required to have a month of bed rest. He called some spiritualist organizations, hoping to obtain a healer or medium for assistance. After trying at the London Spiritual Mission, he was told that a medium named Bo-Goran would come to see him. Don tells what happened then:

"Bo-Goran sat in a chair near the foot of my bed, asked me to relate my experiences, hardly speaking at all himself. After half an hour he insisted that I get up and dress, walk with him down the sixty-eight stairs of the house and along to the Embankment to rest there awhile in the sunshine. Very slowly I crawled from bed, dressed and went out with him. An hour later we returned, had a cup of tea and he left, refusing to accept any fee, or even his fares, and saying I must rest on top of the bed at two o'clock. I would fall into the deepest and most refreshing sleep for some time, rising at six o'clock and feeling like a new born being.

"He could not have been more accurate. I awoke on the stroke of six and felt completely fit and vibrant again. A man of great warmth and compassion, Bo-Goran has been practising first-class mediumship for some forty years, and through my work with the College it has become my privilege to know him"[9]

Paul Beard shed some additional light on the manner in which psychic healing is performed:

Is healing done on a one-to-one basis—that is, with one person attempting the psychic healing and one person receiving it? Or is it done with one person attempting to heal a group? Or with a group attempting to heal one person? Or a group attempting to heal a group? "Most healing is done on a one-to-one basis. It is quite often performed by a group upon patients one by one, when the technique is one of distant healing. One person or a group might attempt to help a situation where perhaps a house appears to be possessed by evil spirits or poltergeistic forces or where it is known that

8. Edwards, *The Power of Healing*, p. 14.
9. Galloway, *Inevitable Journey*, p. 50.

disharmony prevails throughout a family, or within an organisation. In this same sort of context, a group might attempt to heal a group."

What does distance healing entail? Does it have to be performed at a regular time by either the person attempting the healing or the person receiving it? "The essential element entailed in distant healing is an attunement on the healer's part with the benevolent forces that rule the Universe. Attunement can be very swift and healing can be performed at any time, provided the necessary attunement can be obtained. In practice, it is much better for it to be performed at a regular time, both by the person attempting the healing and the person receiving it. The patient sometimes feels aware of an influence at work upon him but his awareness does not condition the healing and is not necessary to it. Many patients respond, though they do not feel anything whilst the healing is taking place. The benefit to the patient in tuning in at a regular time is that this reminds them that they have a part to play also and a responsibility to report to the healers about their condition when required to do so.

"Experience has shown that it is important, except in very unusual cases, such as where healing is given to a baby or to an unconscious or mentally disturbed person, for the patient to assume responsibility for acceptance of the healing treatment. It is all too common for well-meaning persons to ask assistance for dozens of acquaintances without even telling them, and this has little effect. Passing the buck to the healer as the result of vague good will towards ill persons is simply not good enough. At the College, therefore, we only under very special circumstances accept sponsored patients. We consider it far better for the patient to make his own application and assume responsibility for his own reports."

Does the person receiving the healing always know that distance healing is being performed? "Patients vary very greatly in their degree of conscious receptivity. Probably on balance more feel nothing than otherwise, but what does often happen is that a patient reports that although their physical condition is unaltered they themselves have come to feel very differently about it. They often report a feeling of elation or of acceptance or an inner sense of well-being that they did not have before. When this is reported on it is quite likely that physical healing will subsequently follow, either wholly or in part."

Distant healing had been an active part of the work at the College of Psychic Studies but was interrupted by the war problems. However, when the present president, Paul Beard, assumed this position he again introduced healing in 1967. The College believes that the best way to teach distance healing is by the actual performance of it. The theme is that dedication and discipline are the key to performing distant healing, and it is required that those who qualify to perform distant healing concentrate properly on the healing for a half hour weekly, as a minimum, and this done at a specified time.

Harry Edwards, one of the healers mentioned by both Paul Beard and Lawrence LeShan, has been conducting absent healing for over twenty-five years. He believes that if there had been no indications of success, then this type of healing would have simply vanished. Instead, it has steadily increased in scope, as attested to by the fact that his mail for a ten-year period exceeded over half a million letters! In his book *The Evidence For Spirit Healing*, Mr. Edwards tells of over 10,000 cases of healing, which encompass all ages, nationalities, and geographic locations, covering all diseases. He feels that absent healing, so far as the healer is concerned, takes place from thought processes. He believes this is so because "the healing originates from the mental request for healing to reach the patient, and this is the primary factor which sets the healing in motion."[10]

Mr. Edwards holds that this *thought* issued is the common denominator linking all spiritual healing attempts, no matter from what source it may come, or whatever race or religion the healer may be:

"Healings that cannot be medically anticipated take place through people possessing the gift of healing, but differing in their ideas as to the manner of its performance. At our Sanctuary in Shere we have witnessed the healing of people of all religions, not only of Christian denominations but of those subscribing to other religions too—Hindus, Mohammedans and so on—and even of agnostics."[11]

He explains that among religious groups healing is conducted by prayers to God, thus providing the groundwork for intercession. Similarly, spiritualists pray to God and accept healing as divine. However, akin to the concepts described by Paul Beard, they also hold that the true healing agents are go-betweens in "spirit" with whom attunement can be achieved by the healer.

As to how it might be possible for the "spirit" intermediaries to reach someone unknown to the healer and who might live a considerable distance away, Mr. Edwards asserts that although it might be difficult to conceive, it is proved by the high percentage of success. Distance is no problem, and healers have had good results with patients thousands of miles away just as easily as those a few feet away.

Mr. Edwards laments the fact that spiritual healings are mainly gauged by the recovery of those considered incurable, when medicine can no longer help, or in cases where no medical treatment has been sought. Hence, when a patient has received medical treatment as well as the help of a healer, it is exceedingly difficult, if not impossible, to calculate how much credit is due to one or the other.

Equally difficult to ascertain is what the ultimate result of a healing will be. It may be the healer's strongest wish to heal one dear to him and have it prove unsuccessful, only to discover that a stranger with a similar affliction has been healed. It is for this very reason that healers can give no promise that a healing will occur, nor can a time be designated as to when a healing might take place.

In Mr. Edwards' opinion, if a person on the street were asked what would most be of interest to him in the Bible, he would probably say the

10. Edwards, *The Power of Healing*, p. 63.
11. Ibid., pp. 14–15.

miracles of Jesus and the wonders of His healings. Eileen Garrett held a similar view regarding the life and healing ministry of Jesus:
"Even if one applies the most radically destructive criticism to the New Testament . . . and refuses to accept a part of the record in the Gospels as being apostolic (and the apostles were eyewitnesses), yet what remains of the text includes those very accounts of Jesus' healing ministry. His healings were, roughly speaking, of two types: those at which He was personally present and those in which He healed from a distance. But both have this in common, that the obvious motivation in each case was not merely to produce impressive signs and wonders, but was, as healing, an act of love and compassion. And all such healings were done in public or, if circumstances demanded privacy, in close proximity to large numbers of people who could immediately inspect the healed persons and judge for themselves. Nor is it accident that Jesus' favorite and characteristic phrase was 'Be thou whole.' For He knew that wholeness in health, that life alone can truly heal, whether body or mind be ill, or both. And He was the greatest 'unorthodox' healer human history records."[12]

It may be heartening to the reader to hear that the bridge between medical science and faith healing is not as wide as one might think. In 1976, the pharmaceutical firm of Hoffman-LaRoche prepared three educational 45-minute tape recordings called "The Natural Process of Healing," which were mailed by their subsidiary, Roche Laboratories, to over 20,000 physicians and 7,000 psychiatrists requesting copies of the tapes. In talking with Mr. Gerry Manishin, a representative of Roche, I learned that this incredible response from the medical profession occurred after his company mailed 100,000 postcards to doctors offering free to them the tapes of experts, such as psychologist and psychic researcher Dr. Lawrence LeShan, cancer specialist Dr. Carl Simonton, and Dr. A. R. Feinstein, of Yale University School of Medicine, discussing the value of faith healing in the practice of medicine.

And so, there is always hope. The founder of the famous Hallmark Greeting Card Company, Joyce Clyde Hall, after a number of personal setbacks, has followed a philosophy from one of his own cards: "When you get to the end of your rope, tie a knot in it, and hang on."

During the recent visit to America of Leslie Price, Librarian and Member of the Council of the British Society for Psychical Research, he told of his own experience with the "laying on of hands." In addition, he pointed out, "this experience well illustrates the problem of assessment in the psychic field, in particular assessment in psychic healing.

"In 1975, I was simultaneously involved in organizing the Society for Psychical Research study course at short notice and launching *The Christian Parapsychologist.* Anyone who has dealt with printing or publishing knows how horrifying it can be to do a proper job of launching something through the press. It can turn your hair gray. It is equally difficult to set up anything like a study course or a conference, especially during the summer season when people are away on holiday, etc.

12. Garrett, *Life Is the Healer*, pp. 81, 82.

"Both these things were happening to me simultaneously while I was a full-time civil servant. The particular form of stress reaction that I showed was that I lost my voice. And, I lost it on and off for about five or six months.

"In late August 1975, I was able to speak at a symposium on developments in the psychic field at the Annual Conference of the Church's Fellowship for Psychical and Spiritual Studies in England. I was extremely hoarse. I did speak, but my voice was very shaky all that day and I continued to be extremely hoarse. But the following morning, I attended the healing service organized by the Fellowship, taken by the Reverend Chancellor E. Garth Moore, the president of the Fellowship and the Reverend Dr. Martin Israel, Chairman of the Fellowship.

"I was one of many people who went forward for laying on of hands. I received the laying on of hands actually from the Chancellor Garth Moore. After 48 hours, my voice had come back and I never thereafter lost my voice.

"Here comes the problem of assessment. Scientifically, this experience is not presentable as in any way convincing evidence of the reality of paranormal healing. It is personally impressive to me, and I know only too well its practical value because it was extremely inconvenient to say the least to not be able to rely on one's voice and to be rather afraid when the phone rang that one would not be able to make oneself comprehended by the person at the other end. So, I know how important this experience was to me.

"But, equally do I know that scientifically I have no hope at all of presenting this as evidence of healing, because it could be argued that most throat disorders clear up after a certain period of time. I was also receiving a certain amount of medication. It wasn't particularly effective. I had an appointment for the first time to see a throat specialist a couple of weeks afterwards and it could be argued that the possibility of receiving specialist treatment stimulated the healing forces inside me."

I asked Leslie what he would suggest to people who might be thousands of miles away from a healing group such as the one he attended, as to where they should go or from whom they might seek help in this area. Leslie offered these suggestions:

"If people are particularly interested in healing, if they are religious people, I would advise them to work through their own denomination. In most of the main denominations there are fellowships and organizations that are particularly active in promoting the healing ministry.

"If a person is of a nonreligious temperament and interested in healing, I would suggest as a starting point contact with the parapsychological bodies which are researching healing: The American Society for Psychical Research Education Department in New York, and in England the Health for the New Age Trust is an active resource center on information on healing and can give details of practical avenues of service in the healing area.

"I think that the simplest way to learn healing or to explore healing if you feel that you are called to be a healer is to try it. To begin privately and discreetly by sending out healing prayers for relatives and friends afflicted with quite simple disorders. Do this simply and discreetly without even mentioning it, without in any way making it public and just see what happens. Most public libraries today have at least a reasonable section on such matters as healing and there are several very good introductions to the healing area such as *An Outline of Spiritual Healing*, by Gordon Turner, *The Healing Touch*, by M. H. Tester, and also the works of Olga Worrall."

And so here, again, we hear the name of Olga Worrall. Because I wanted to witness firsthand the type of healing given by Olga Worrall, my husband and I attended one of the weekly healing services held at the Mount Washington United Methodist Church in Baltimore, known as the New Life Clinic. Ambrose Worrall also performed his healing ministry here before he passed away. I felt it would be a disservice to the reader to try to encompass a description into a brief paragraph, and for that reason, I have chosen to devote the next chapter in its entirety to Olga Worrall and the New Life Clinic. Examples of healing accomplished will be given, as well as descriptions of healing done over great distances, which Olga tells about in an informal interview.

CHAPTER

4

Healing Hands at the New Life Clinic

How can I truly describe the kindness and the warmth generated by the healers at the New Life Clinic in Baltimore? Is there a way I can adequately convey how the touch of such devoted healing hands brings a joy and a warmth to your being which is not soon forgotten? When I visited these healing services for the first time, there were five healers, acting as a literal "battery," charging energy through their "laying on of hands." On this particular day, after the services held at the Mount Washington United Methodist Church, I spoke with four of the healers: Dr. Robert Kirkley, minister of the church; Dr. Robert Leichtman, M.D.; Lynn Brallier, M.S.N., Director of a Crisis Intervention Service in Washington, D.C.; and Dr. Olga Worrall, author, lecturer, psychic, and healer.

At 10:00, on a Thursday morning, Olga Worrall spoke, and approximately 300 people listened. They listened to Olga telling them to leave their religious denominations "out on the lawn" and later to observe a short period of "Quaker silence" in order to be receptive, for "it is only in the stillness that we can hear the whispering of God." Following the silent period, and after a short service conducted by Dr. Kirkley, all visitors were invited to come to the altar for the "laying on of hands." The hushed movements of those kneeling at the rail and the desires of the many in distress—in arm casts, or having other visible physical afflictions—created a surge of hope and energy which engulfed the entire group within this little church.

You *know* that something very special is happening here. It is a very personal experience, yet shared with many; one cannot help but feel uplifted. When you leave the front doors of this sanctuary, a great weight is left behind, almost as if you had been told, "Come, you can leave your heavy burden here—it is much too heavy to carry."

There are, of course, many skeptics among the group. Probably one of the best examples would be Lynn Brallier, now one of the New Life Clinic healers, who first came there not as a healer but seeking to be healed.

Actually, Lynn was literally pushed to Olga Worrall and the New Life

Clinic by a friend. Lynn had been in a terrible automobile accident and had been hit broadside by another car. Three years prior to this accident, surgery had been performed with a spinal fusion two places in her neck because of degeneration of the disks. It appeared to the surgeon that the next two disks up would also have to be replaced with hip bone, but he was reluctant to proceed because the surgery would be too radical. It would have meant one solid piece of bone, which could easily fracture and sever the spinal cord. Therefore, the surgeon treated Lynn very conservatively, with bed rest and drugs, including codeine for the pain she was in constantly.

After six weeks of bed rest, and feeling no better, she was told by her surgeon that there was no hope for any relief from the pain for several months. Shortly thereafter, a friend brought Lynn the transcript of a meeting of the Academy of Parapsychology and Medicine. It seemed ridiculous to Lynn at the time that her friend should have given her this. She only knew a little bit about what was called "faith healing," and she felt it was simply some sort of psychological trick, but she appreciated her friend's interest in her. When reading the part that Olga had written, Lynn's reaction was that she was "somebody weird that I wouldn't want to meet. She was much too far-out religious for me. I had thrown out the Christianity kind of business that I had grown up in when I went to college and decided I was really a Buddhist at heart." However, after being urged by her friend to at least give the New Life Clinic a try, Lynn agreed, thinking that "at least I would be out of bed and it would be entertaining and probably one of the better 'shows' and would give me something to laugh at."

Lynn's husband, who is a doctor, was very much against her going to the healing services. He was concerned because he knew Lynn had very little faith in such things, and because he didn't want her to suffer disappointment. However, Lynn decided there would be no harm in visiting the clinic and proceeded to arrange the trip.

When arriving at the church, Lynn fully expected Olga to appear in "flying robes" and that she would be shouting hysterically. But, "Olga was dressed very sanely in a dress." Trained as a psychotherapist, Lynn kept looking for signs of hysteria or psychotic behavior in Olga. She could not believe that healing could possibly take place in this atmosphere. "Then when the healing service started, I really freaked out. I couldn't believe that people would walk up to a rail, have someone touch them, and think this was going to heal them."

Lynn was adamantly against going up to the altar for laying on of hands, but her friend's persistent urging continued and she finally agreed to do so. "Olga put her hands one on either side of my head. Then, probably five or six seconds after she had her hands on my head, I felt this tremendous heat going down into my neck and into my back. Then she took her hands away, and the heat dissipated." It surprised Lynn greatly that this could happen by somebody merely touching her, more so because she had no expectations. In fact, she was so amazed at the experience that she did not realize until quite some time after leaving the church that her pain had disappeared.

Previously she had been wearing a neck brace and an arm sling. She could hardly move her right arm, and because of the agonizing pain, her arm had to be propped up on a box while driving. As she drove away from the church, she suddenly realized her arm no longer had to be propped up, and that it was moving freely, without pain. At first, as a psychotherapist, she was looking for some other explanation—hysteria, or shock. But when the absence of pain persisted, Lynn realized that there was "something else" involved.

That evening, when her husband met her, he growled, "Well, did you get healed in that place?" Lynn threw her arm out in a gesture she heretofore had been unable to do without causing tears from the pain. Her husband was astonished, and Lynn retorted, as she flung her arm out, "Did I get healed! Of course I got healed. What did you think I went there for?" However, they both knew that was not the reason she had gone and they both fully expected the pain to come back the next morning. "But that was a year and a half ago," Lynn proudly proclaimed, and "after another couple of visits to the Clinic, I was as well as I had been before the accident."

When Lynn went back to see her surgeon, he was equally flabbergasted. He had offered to help her lift her arm during the examination, but Lynn showed him that she could raise her arm and move it quite freely. He then offered to help support Lynn's head while she moved it back, but she assured him she did not need the assistance. It was plain that Lynn would not be needing the radical surgery after all.

At the New Life Clinic I asked a medical doctor, Robert Leichtman, what he was "doing here today?" He replied, "I am here to participate in the healing services, and to do what I can to heal people through unorthodox means rather than the standard medical treatment, and to some degree this is apparently effective."

Dr. Leichtman, who recently spoke before the National Institute of Health in Bethesda about perspective on spiritual healing, believes that often a person will exhibit psychic potential as well as healing gifts, but cautions they should never be confused. He stresses they are two distinct operations, like "listening and hearing, versus speech." Dr. Leichtman explains that the healing work is something which he has done informally for a long time, and the healing attitude is one of having a compassionate interest in people.

"As a physician, many people come to me who need my help psychologically and/or physically. The real healing energies are those which emanate from one's very spirit, that is, the immortal soul. This is what heals. This is what heals each individual and this is what the true spiritual healer must use to work on other people. My concept of this is that our 'higher self,' which is a psychological term, is identical with what is called the 'soul' in religion. That is, the immortal essence. And this is the repository of wisdom that nurtures the intellectual capacity of the personality. The soul is the repository of the love and joy that is the nurturing energy behind our feelings, and it is the health and vitality behind the physical form and function."

Talking of a "Universal Current" that generates psychic energy, Dr. Leichtman explained that "it is like getting your house wired for electricity and then you are ready to cook and to heat your house and air condition, and do a number of things as well as illuminate it. But there is no guarantee that just because the electric company has wired your house and hooked you up to the main terminal that any of these things are going to happen. That requires a great deal of effort to understand how to work the mechanisms. And I am referring here to the counterpart of knowing how to turn on and use your stove, your TV set, your mixmaster, your dishwasher, and so on. In terms of the healer, this means the healer must learn his or her mind and emotional equipment and physical body in order to transmit energies of the soul—or light of the soul, if you will—through himself and then to the person who might be coming for healing."

In Dr. Leichtman's view, the healing force works through the mind and emotions and then the physical body: "Some people ask why is it that some people are healed and some people are not." The first reason would be that "perhaps the healer is not a very good healer." But assuming one is a good healer, "the second thing one tends to see is that there is great psychological conflict and distress, and this is blocking the healing activities. It is either blocking it or the very patterns of the disease are tied up in the mind and emotions of that person and, until those patterns are removed, physical healings by and large will not be complete."

When giving a "proper healing," according to Dr. Leichtman, "some effort has to be given to cleansing the mind and the emotions before the physical healing can occur. Sometimes a physical healing can be effected, but [the sickness] will be recreated after the healing because the pattern for disease and distress still lies within the mind and therefore all levels need to be approached." In his view, the physically unhealthy have a very difficult block in their mind and emotions which prevents the healing life of their soul from penetrating into the physical form.

One wonders if there might not be a third possibility as to why a healing does or does not take place. The two possibilities indicated above are that the healer may not be a good one, or that the person seeking to be healed has strong psychological blocks against the healing. Let's take the "electricity" concept one step further. Couldn't it also be possible that the healer and the person to be healed are on different energy impulses, much as one might say, "The chemistry doesn't mix."

For example, when a person needs a blood transfusion of Type A blood, Type B won't work. It is only when the correct blood type is obtained that the transfusion can take place. When the healer has all the prerequisites for transfusing energy, it may not be purely a psychological block on the part of the patient which prevents healing from occurring. It may simply be that the healer is Type A blood, or energy, when Type B is required for the "healing transfusion." And just as God has given us all different types of blood, so may this apply to the energies received from the Universal Current.

Perhaps a way of discerning whether such "healing energies" are Type A, Type B, etc., might prove possible through a study of color. If the energies emanating from a healer can be translated into color (the aura of the healer), a comparison could then be made with the color (aura) emanating from the healee. Color experiments of this nature might determine if color compatibility of "aura types" has any bearing on the ultimate outcome of an attempted healing. Just as specific types of blood are needed for a transfusion to take place, similarly there may be specific "aura types" which would permit a transfusion of healing energies to occur. If so, color could prove to be a key in determining when a healing will or will not take place. (In the next chapter you will read more about auras and the importance of color in diagnosis and healing.)

I later talked with Dr. Robert Kirkley, the former minister of the Mount Washington United Methodist Church. Through his efforts a healing practice was established there. I asked him what he would recommend to those people who are isolated and far away from areas where healing services are held, and how they could help themselves. He advised that they should read books on healing, like the work of Ambrose and Olga Worrall and Harold Sherman, and then to go into the "meditative state themselves and work on their own bodies and minds."

When asked if there are any pitfalls in psychic experiences, Dr. Kirkley warned "many people get psychically involved before they are spiritually or emotionally prepared to handle the psychic experiences. For example, a woman spoke to me after the Clinic today. She had just been coming out of a period of strong depression, and she said, however, that when she went to bed at night, she was *aware* that there were forces in the room that were not good for her and what were they? I said, well, they could be the thoughts of people. They could be the emotions of others. They could be some psychic or spiritual visitors. We do live in a spiritual universe. We are surrounded constantly by spiritual beings. Not all of them are helpful. Some of them are looking to us. They want to draw our energies. They want to draw our thoughts. Some of them are earthbound and are looking for ways to express themselves and they need our bodies to do this. So, we do have to be on guard against this. I remember an old saying that 'An open mind, like an open door, needs screens to keep the bugs out.' "

It was in the lovely and serene atmosphere of Olga Worrall's home that I learned of the many thousands of letters she has received regarding the distance healing and absentee healing she conducts both at the Clinic and every night at her 9:00 prayer time. Olga reserves 9:00 until 9:05 P.M. for those who cannot meet her personally, but who can join in prayer with her from a distance for five minutes every evening. Olga asks that prayer, whether it be aloud or silently, be prayed just prior to 9:00 P.M. and then, at 9:00, all praying halt, "and that conscious awareness of the Divine Presence be sought for the five minutes by anticipating in expectancy some revelation, by intuition or sensing, of the actual demonstration of Divine Power."

With regard to the 9:00 P.M. prayer time, I asked Olga when people in other parts of the world should pray. She replied: "People from France and other parts of the world sit at 9:00 their time and have written of so many things happening." She maintains that no one's rest should be disturbed to stay up until 2:00 A.M. in the morning to equate the 9:00 P.M. hour in the United States because "in God's world, there is no time."

Olga tells of the many thousands who have written, saying, "Tumors have disappeared. Heart conditions were improved. Children who were in comas have revived. They are just too numerous to mention. People that write in, in faith—who are not just fooling around—they join me every night at 9:00 and then they write to say that cancer has disappeared, etc. Now, that doesn't mean everybody is going to get rid of cancer joining every night." Olga doesn't know why one healing will occur in one individual and not in another. But, she strongly urges patience; that continued prayer at 9:00 has brought forth letters telling of healings from all over the world—not just from Baltimore—"from as far away as Australia." When I exclaimed, "Then, this can work over thousands of miles?," Olga smiled and replied: "There is no distance in God's world."

Citing an example, Olga related a story of one of her healings:

"I was in Japan and I was giving a workshop in the Grand Heights Air Force Base in Tokyo. A young man came into the meeting. No one knew who he was. He had a very badly swollen knee. After the meeting was over, still not identifying him, his wife asked me if I could do anything for his badly swollen knee. I said I didn't know, but I would try. I touched, but nothing happened. That night, they had an earthquake in Tokyo. It was 2:00 in the morning, but no one seemed to be getting excited about it. They have them all the time. So, I thought, well you just stay in bed if you have an earthquake when you're in Tokyo! And, while I was laying there, I thought to myself, well, I may as well make good use of this time. And, I began to think of absent healing and suddenly this young man's face appeared right before me. And I projected the healing energy into his leg, into the badly swollen knee, and I just held the thought that God's healing is manifesting in that young man's knee. And, then I went off to sleep very quickly. Well, the next night, he called the base, quite excited and this was the story he told. He awakened at about 2:00 in the morning, burning up and no one in his right mind is ever hot in Tokyo, especially at night. He asked his wife to open up the window but she said she wouldn't because she was all bundled up. So, he got out of bed, got his crutches, walked over to the window and opened it up. He got back into bed and as he was lying there, he saw me standing right in the room! When he recognized me, suddenly he had a terrific pain in the knee and his knee gave a wild jerk and instantly the swelling was completely gone. No pain, and he could move his knee in every position. This was the story he told us. Then we asked who he was and he was the head of surgery at the air force base right next to our base."

A man with a severe eye injury caused by an accident with an acetylene torch was brought to the Worralls. The man had been told by his physician that virtually all vision had been lost and that he should learn Braille. Ambrose Worrall described what happened:

"Olga gave him healing through the laying on of hands; we held him in our thoughts during the nine o'clock prayer hour, which Olga and I continued in the evenings in our home. This man began to gain his vision again, in the lower section of the eye. Gradually, this strengthened to a point where he could see."[1]

During my interview with Olga I asked how one should pray—if the prayer should be spontaneous or at a specified time.

"Both," she said. "You should pray when the spirit moves you, quietly and not make a big issue about it. It is often a good discipline to take, say, five minutes when everything is quiet and go off and sit in the silence and just sit quietly. It is good for the soul. When you feel moved to say a prayer, just saying 'Thank you, God' is a beautiful prayer.

"Everybody can say a *few* words! So, just say a few words. Then be quiet. Don't broadcast any more. When you are broadcasting, you can't receive. My mother, who was a Catholic, used to warn us, 'Don't pray the ears off God. Don't say a lot of unnecessary words because God is busy.' That was her way of telling us to be precise in what we were going to pray about."

What if one wanted to pray to help someone else's situation? What could they do in conjunction with their prayers?

"This should be a positive prayer," Olga explained. "It should be a prayer of *knowing*. For example, if it is your husband, you would say, 'Thank you, God, for the healing of my husband,' and then mention whatever the problem is." Olga stated this should be prayed as if it were already accomplished: "You should anticipate and already feel that it is taking place."

What would Olga say to someone who wanted to heal themselves? "Exactly the same thing they do at 9:00 P.M. when they join me in prayer. They sit quietly, they say a prayer to cleanse the mind, to put them in the proper state, and then just say, 'Thank you God for the healing of whatever the problem is,' and then sit quietly for a few minutes. Do that every night and when you are *ready* to receive that healing and *know* how to handle it, it will come into its own. I have had people tell me for months they sat and nothing happened, and then suddenly one night a tremendous healing came over them, because they stuck to it, and didn't become discouraged."

Can a healer heal himself? "A healer can, and does heal himself," says Olga, "unless the illness is too great and needs proper medical attention; and even then, the healer can shorten the time needed to complete a healing."

Many letters and statements regarding personal experiences of healings appear in the Worralls' book, *The Miracle Healers*, formerly entitled *The Gift of Healing*, including some moving accounts of healings that occurred at the New Life Clinic:

"With hundreds of individuals coming to the Wednesday services, or writing and asking to be remembered in prayers by Olga and myself . . . many healings resulted, too many indeed even to begin to describe all of

1. Worrall, *The Miracle Healers*, p. 120.

them. They covered every range of illness. Healings occurred right at the altar in some instances, during the administration of the laying on of hands, and prayer.

"A woman came to the clinic to pray one morning, the day before she was to be operated on for removal of a growth on her eye. When she arrived at the doctor's office the following day, the physician, with great amazement, informed her that the growth that was to have required serious eye surgery had become so loose he was able to lift it off with a pair of tweezers.

"A brain tumor operation was called off by a surgeon only a few hours before it was to have taken place because tests indicated the tumor had disappeared. The man involved had been 'preparing' himself for this operation by attending sessions at the Clinic and coming to the church regularly for prayer.

"A case of considerable importance involved a high official of one of the major-league ball clubs who had a growth on his throat that had been diagnosed as cancerous. When he came to the altar for healing, Olga placed her hands on his neck: her left hand on the front part of his throat, the right hand on the back. She held her fingers in this position for a few moments, and felt what she described later as a tingling sensation go through her hands. At the same moment the man himself looked up and said, 'I feel terrific heat going into my throat.' "[2]

On the following Wednesday, Olga was asked by the baseball executive to again place her hands on his neck, because his throat seemed so improved. He also indicated he had an appointment after the service with a doctor who was a specialist in cancer. Olga again placed her hands on his throat, and the man once again felt intense heat flowing from her fingers into his throat.

"That night" the account continues, "there was an evening service at the church. Dr. Day, [minister of the Mt. Vernon Place Methodist Church] was in his office just prior to this service when a man barged into the office, thoroughly distraught. It was the cancer specialist. He demanded of Dr. Day, 'What have you done with my patient?'

"Dr. Day was frightened. He did not know what had happened. Further, the Johns Hopkins specialist was a member of the board of the Mt. Vernon Place Methodist Church. He then proceeded to tell Dr. Day that the patient had come to him following a session of the New Life Clinic and that the cancer which had been the size of a half dollar was gone and all that remained was a scar about as thin as a thread.

"The growth did not return. The baseball man at the last report we had was retired and living happily in Florida."[3]

After a grant from the Department of Health, Education, and Welfare to Johns Hopkins University, Olga Worrall was called upon to speak to their School of Hygiene and Public Health on the spiritual healing process. While appearing on the Beverly Sills Show in New York, Olga was asked if

2. Ibid., pp. 118, 119.
3. Ibid., p. 119.

everyone had this talent. Olga replied yes, but some have more than others. Explaining that while she herself could sing, and did sing in the church choir, Beverly Sills had a far greater talent for singing.

In a recent issue of the Smithsonian magazine, an article pertaining to auras featured Kirlian photography of Olga's hands, showing the healing energies that could be seen emanating from them. In the summer of 1976 the Smithsonian Institute sponsored a traveling exhibit on psychic phenomena—the first of its kind ever to be circulated by that prestigious organization—established as an educational program to the public. The unique exhibit underscored examples of scientific cases involving psychic phenomena, including psychic healing. Dr. Margaret Mead, the famous anthropologist, author, and lecturer, wrote introductory comments for the exhibit in the hope it would clarify psychic research, one of which states, "The whole history of scientific advancement is full of scientists investigating phenomena that 'the establishment' did not believe were there."

The sincerity and warmth of this very caring healer is felt by all around her. The type of response brought when people realize a genuine desire to help, and when it is seen that the sincerity is real, was told by Olga's late husband Ambrose Worrall:

"The response to this clinic was startling to many in the church. Olga and I had long since learned how quickly the word spreads, how hungry the world is for this kind of healing, how people reach out to something they can believe, something obviously not for profit or personal aggrandizement, not sham but truly healing."[4]

Olga performs her healing at the New Life Clinic of the Mt. Washington United Methodist Church in Baltimore and not at her home. For her healing ministry, she accepts no money, love offerings, or gifts of any type. But with the tons of letters she receives, Olga does admit that when people do not enclose stamped, self-addressed envelopes for her reply, that this is "added work."

I asked Olga what the many people who might like to find out about healing services within their own area could do:

"I would suggest that they go and bombard the church doors, and knock the doors down, and insist that their churches have healing services. The mandate of the church to a minister is to go out and teach, preach, and heal. It is the responsibility of the church to conduct healing services— sensible healing services that won't be filling the people with a lot of guilt complexes and fears, and to work in cooperation with the medical profession. As I always maintain, the medical doctor is the physician of the physical body and the minister, priest, rabbi, is the physician of the spiritual body, and the two of them have to heal the whole man."

In closing this chapter on the New Life Clinic, I would like to say a little prayer of my own: "Thank you, God. Thank you for all your healers."

4. Ibid., p. 115.

CHAPTER

5

Aura Readings

The aura has been defined as a circular atmosphere, sometimes invisible, sometimes distinctive, which surrounds the head of an individual. Whether seen or not, the aura is always present. The aura can be likened to the nimbus, or halo, which medieval and Renaissance artists painted around the heads of saints, holy persons, and kings.

One of the foremost aura psychics of our times, Eileen J. Garrett, claimed the aura she "saw" was a foglike atmosphere that emanated from the body like a field of energy. Judith Richardson Haimes, the well-known aura-reading psychic, describes the aura very succinctly: "When you look at me, you see my hair. When I look at you, I see your aura."

What do aura-reading psychics see? They generally claim to see a rainbow of colors surrounding the head. These colors range from deep red through blue, green, and yellow to pale gold and violet.

In a recent interview with Judith Richardson Haimes, she described the colors in some detail: "People who see auras as I do are able to see auras in a . . . spectrum of colors—10, 12, 15 colors at once. . . . When I see an aura, I see little dots, little flecks of color; how much there is; how little there is; what it's next to; how it is shaped; what shades the colors are in. . . . Every single color has a meaning."

Judith claims that no one person has an aura of just one color—say, all of blue. When she is reading a person's aura, she can see about fifty different shades of blue. Each shade has its own meaning, ranging from a dark Ming blue (deep emotional scars) to a pale "innocent" blue (peace of mind). In between there is a turquoise blue, representing dependency on alcohol or drugs.

Eileen Garrett believed yellow denoted a vital force. Further, she claimed a yellow-green aura surrounded the head of the forcefully intelligent and the intellectual: "I must adhere to my point that when I see yellow in the aura—the most luminous color in the spectrum, lying between bright orange and green—it denotes superior intelligence and power."[1]

1. Garrett, *Many Voices*, pp. 234–35.

In her visits to hospitals, Eileen claimed she saw deep-brown auras around the sick and ailing—and that gray auras almost always hung over the heads of patients dying of cancer. In many of her aura readings, Eileen diagnosed approaching illness through a darkening color field which appeared at the place on the human body where the illness would occur. She stated the colors would darken and glow drably—*while their force and intensity* would slowly diminish.

The *Handbook of Psychic Discoveries* offers a brief historical review of healing energy and the aura:

"The concept of an energy body and of an aura, which has come down to us from the ancient sciences of the Far East and India, has formed a part of the doctrine of many groups that have made a study of these Oriental and Indian writings, i.e. the Theosophists and Rosicrucians. Swami Sivanada describes the Hindu and Yogic theory of *Prana*—the universal energy considered more basic than atomic energy, 'Whatever moves, works or has life is but an expression or manifestation of Prana. . . . Prana is the link between the astral (or auric) and the physical body. When the slender threadlike Prana (the silver cord) is cut off, the astral body separates from the physical body. Death takes place. . . .' The Prana aura surrounding the body is said to be the means by which one person may impart healing energy to another by magnetic healing."[2]

Can a person's well-being be helped by having the aura read? Judith Richardson Haimes answers: "It can absolutely be helped. When you say, 'You have a bundle of creativity—channel it' or, 'You have a chemical imbalance causing great depression—have it checked out by an endocrinologist.' There is no end to the things that can be done by seeing the aura."

Judith cited an example of a twenty-four-year-old woman who came to see her. Judith saw in her aura that there was a cancer present, and from the aura read that the girl would be dead by November if the problem was not acted upon immediately. Because she felt so certain of this aura reading, Judith informed the girl of her findings.

Dr. Julian Millman, an obstetrician-gynecologist in the Philadelphia area, documents subsequent events, after this patient was referred to him on October 3, 1974:

"The patient gave me a history of a Pap Smear Class 3 following which she had a cervical conization done on September 3, 1974, which showed Epidermoid Carcinoma in Situ. The cancer was confined to the cervix and according to the pathology report, it would seem the patient had been cured by the conization. After this, the patient was seen by Judith, who strongly felt there was a malignancy present. I conducted a routine pap smear and it was negative for any malignant cells. However, because Carcinoma in Situ could very well become a serious problem later on, and since the woman already had three children, I believed the uterus should come out. So I operated on this young lady because of the possibility of malignancy. Upon removal of the uterus, it showed it to have a Carcinoma

2. Ostrander and Schroeder, *Handbook of Psychic Discoveries*, p. 50.

in Situ with micro invasion, which meant that if she had been left alone, this could have developed into a full-blown metastatic carcinoma which could very well have caused her demise.

"At one time I was quite skeptical about Judith's abilities in connection with being able to detect medical problems through reading the aura, but I have grown less skeptical. I have found, in working with Judith, that she is 85 percent accurate in her findings, which is more than many doctors can claim."

Judith also puts her aura-reading talents to work helping psychiatrists and psychologists. "They will bring me a photograph of an individual they have had for at least six months' evaluation. I will take four or five minutes and read the photograph just for its psychological nature. So far, ten out of ten have been correct. . . . What I saw, it took the psychologist and the psychiatrist four to six months to evaluate. By doing this, we are hoping to eventually be able to cut down a great deal of the evaluation time—thereby getting people on their feet much sooner."

Judith accomplishes the same thing with physical illnesses: "A person will often show illnesses physically in the aura prior to a medical test being able to show this or before any symptoms show themselves. Often, I have sent an individual to have a metabolism checked—or this or that checked—because of a weakness in the aura . . . only to find out they had no symptoms, they felt wonderful, yet the doctor found early stages of a serious illness."

Judith often uses her aura-reading ability to work with the police, and has volunteered twenty to forty hours a week, for which she doesn't charge a fee. "They bring me a photograph of the victim before the crime," she said, explaining how she works. "They tell me nothing. I tell them what I see. The police may have clues 2, 4, and 6. If what I tell them fits in, then the rest of what I tell them on the individual gives them enough to investigate more deeply." Then, given a photograph taken at the scene of the crime, she pieces together from the photograph what has happened. Judith claims that when an individual goes through a *strong* emotion, the imprint of the aura is much *stronger*. Therefore, if a person is murdered, the imprint is going to carry more force. Also, she advises, the murderer is going to be giving off a *strong* emotional fury so that the assailant's aura is also very strong.

When Judith is finished, she has literally "thrown a box of 1,000 puzzle pieces upside down on a table. Since they already have the edge of the puzzle put together, all they do is take these bits and pieces and place it together." What Judith provides in the way of information will not, of course, hold up in a court, she states. However, what the police will do is "take what I have given them and explore and, finding evidence, can then bring it into court."

A number of psychic persons who "see" and "read" auras claim the human aura is composed of many colors and shades—depending upon the health or emotions of the individual. They see it as several pulsating, misty bands of color surrounding the head and body of individuals. The first band seems to project about one-half inch from the body. After that, there is a second auric band extending about three or four inches. It is this "inner" aura that stands out in the most brilliant colors—or in the case of illness, the darkest and drabbest. A third aura, extending out some eight to ten inches, is the misty and pulsating shape that many people—not just psychics—claim to see. Many aura readers have likened the aura to heat waves rising up from a hot pavement or boiling water.

Judith Richardson Haimes sees "about five superimposed layers." She explains what she sees in each:

"You have what that individual is born with, what their traits are— indications towards positive, negative; if they are going to be highly creative or have a terrible temper, or very selfish or very giving; then you have as that individual grows different things or events that take place in the life of that individual, which is a pretty good indication of how these other traits are going to develop, whether positive or negative. Then, you have what the individual is today. Then you have the projection forward; then you have the emotions that are going on presently as you are reading them. So, you have a constantly changing aura in front of you. And that is why, as an aura-reading psychic, when I read an individual, I have to wade through a couple of layers of the aura so I can make sure the person isn't just upset sitting across from me today, or just had an argument with their spouse."

Ambrose Worrall, the renowned psychic healer, relates how his wife, Olga, saw auras:

"She could see people's auras, emanations in various colors around a person, sometimes gold or white, sometimes blue, sometimes, when the individual was in anger or despair, red or deep brown verging into black or blue-black.

"The first aura she was to see, in fact, was her own. As she relates this, she was perhaps five or six years old, and would climb upon a chair and . . . gaze into the mirror at herself and her aura. She did not call it her aura because she had never heard the word. To Olga she was looking at her 'ghost.' That was what she called these colored emanations that ran like a nimbus around her reflection."[3]

After the death of her infant brother, which Olga, who was clairvoyant, had predicted, she was frightened and didn't want to see her ghost in the mirror any longer. Because she was afraid, she stayed away from the mirror. After some years had passed, and her fears had diminished somewhat, she decided to look once more into the gilded-frame mirror. Upon doing so, she no longer saw her "ghost" in it. Ambrose writes of the incident: "Perhaps the fact that she had not looked for all these years had something to do with it; perhaps these are gifts that die if unused. In any case Olga to this writing has not seen her own aura again in the glass. Occasionally, particularly in healing situations, she does see auras around other individuals."[4]

Such early psychic experiences sadly can cause a great deal of anxiety

3. Worrall, *The Miracle Healers*, p. 76.
4. Ibid., p. 76.

and fear for both the child experiencing her psychic powers for the first time and for the parents, who don't know precisely what is happening or how to respond. Ambrose Worrall explains:

"Episodes are usually difficult and emotionally disruptive for both child and parent because so often the parent has no idea what is happening; he tries to tell the child that it is all his imagination, or that he is merely making things up to attract attention, or that he is mentally ill and should see a doctor. He is told, in the kindest way, that no one is there, in any case; or that it is something frightening and bad and the child becomes terrified of the dark. None of this is the parents' fault; they simply do not know how to react to the psychic child; it is a part of our education that has yet to be understood and developed.

"Because of this, many sensitives, as children, are put through needless anguish by well-meaning adults who do not understand"[5]

Many psychics have expressed a similar concern that people are raised to be afraid or ashamed of their feelings, and most feel that by accepting and experiencing these psychic feelings, one can deal with them better.

Thus, along with the colors of the aura, similarly a myriad of complexities surround the subject of ESP and psychic phenomena. It is hoped that no roads will be barred to us in the quest to discover, to experience, and to understand causes of psychic happenings as well as their chemistry and mechanics.

5. Ibid., p. 74.

PART II

The Trail Leads to ESP

When I was eleven years old, blowing out the candles on my birthday cake, I suddenly "saw" that my grandfather would be taken ill. I saw around him Halloween decorations of pumpkins, witches, and black cats. Then I could not see my grandfather's face any longer. Ten days later, it came to pass that none of us could see his face—he died on Halloween.

Because I literally saw my grandfather's death ten days before it occurred and since he was not ill and no one had any expectation of it, this was precognition—an event "seen" before it actually happens.

Precognition is one part of ESP. But what does extrasensory perception mean?

Scientifically, it means a sense beyond the five that we normally possess. It means something extra ordinary, something special, something unique.

And yet I have discovered that, quite to the contrary, most people possess it.

This does not mean that we possess it to the same degree as some of the great and gifted psychics, but it does mean that you and I—the average person—have had and can have experiences that are extraordinarily beyond the usually accepted five senses.

How many of us have had the following type of experience happen:

One afternoon I was en route home via subway, carrying a heavy, cumbersome package. While on the train, I thought to myself how nice it would be if a neighbor of mine would appear at the subway exit so that I could be relieved of the heavy parcel. As I climbed up the stairway out onto the street, I looked up to find my neighbor standing just in front of me, almost as if he had received my "wishful thinking" that he be there. Happily, he took my package and carried it home for me.

For those of you who have had experiences of this nature, they are called "telepathic" communications and are also a part of ESP.

In another incident, one afternoon in a taxi, I suddenly "saw" that in the vicinity of our destination there had been an accident involving another taxi. I told the driver of my taxi that we should take another route because

I thought traffic would be jammed up, but the driver insisted that this would not be so. Approximately ten minutes later, as we were approaching the address I had given the driver, we saw that a taxi had hit a lamppost after going out of control. And traffic had been backed up for several blocks.

This was an instance of clairvoyance.

Let's look at another example of precognition, to help clarify the difference between it and clairvoyance:

One November afternoon in 1965 my husband telephoned from his office to say he planned to stop and buy some Christmas cards before taking the train home. Shortly after hanging the phone up, I sensed a great danger to my husband and "saw" only total blackness. Alarmed, I telephoned him back and said under no circumstances to stop for the Christmas cards but to come home right away. No sooner had he turned his key in our front door than there was a complete blackout and all electricity in parts of the East went out, leaving hundreds of thousands stranded in trains, elevators, and buildings.

Extraordinary sensory perception—ESP—is made up of many particular talents, the most common of which are telepathy, precognition, clairvoyance, psychometry, and psychokinesis (sometimes referred to as telekinesis).

An abbreviated and simplified explanation to help you understand these talents is given below:

ESP of someone's thoughts is TELEPATHY.

ESP of seeing visually events or things is CLAIRVOYANCE.

ESP of knowing the future is called PRECOGNITION.

ESP of feeling objects is known as PSYCHOMETRY.

ESP of moving objects is PSYCHOKINESIS.

But they are *all* forms of ESP.

The study of extrasensory perception (ESP) that lies beyond the scope of orthodox psychologists is called parapsychology. Hence the researchers engaged in this work presently are called parapsychologists. In the late nineteenth centruy, Sir William Crookes, the eminent British physicist, chose the name "psychic" for a new force, in order to distinguish it from the other forces of nature. It followed that those studying this force at that time were called psychic researchers.

Let us now proceed on the adventurous trail of ESP and its many talents.

6

Telepathy

One evening, a short time after I had moved to New York, I felt an urgent need to telephone my mother in Texas. I kept "hearing" popping sounds and they alarmed me—as if my mother were in danger. My sister, who was living with me, felt we should exercise caution with regard to an astronomical telephone bill, and indicated that if the feeling persisted by morning, I could call then.

The next morning, while I did not feel the same sense of urgency, I still felt there had been a problem of some sort. Upon telephoning my mother, I learned that the previous evening she had been asked to help cashier in my uncle's liquor store because an employee was ill. The store was held up, and the robbers, just before leaving, began shooting at all the bottles. Mother ducked under the counter, thus escaping harm, but said she kept hearing the "popping" of the bottles.

How is telepathy defined? In all my readings about the subject of telepathy, one of the best definitions I have come across is the following one by David Hammond: "Telepathy is the awareness of the thoughts, impressions, and mental states of another person."[1] Simple, yet very profound.

Another excellent definition, which complements the above, is that given by Andrea Fodor Litkei, well-known author and lecturer, and daughter of the noted parapsychologist and psychoanalyst, Dr. Nandor Fodor: "Telepathy is the transmission of thoughts independently of the recognised channels of the sense."[2]

These definitions tell us that one person has knowledge of the thoughts and impressions of another person and that this knowledge occurs simultaneously with the thoughts and impressions of that person. In other words, A knows what B is thinking at the time that B is actually thinking it.

1. Hammond, *The Search for Psychic Power*, p. 8.
2. Litkei, *ESP: An Account of the Fabulous in Our Everyday Lives*, p. 20.

Is the physical distance between the sender and the receiver of telepathic communications of any consequence? Telepathy can occur in the same room, in the next room, one mile away, or one thousand miles away. Distance does not seem to be a barrier. However, researchers are still investigating this question.

When did the term "telepathy" make its first appearance? How is telepathy different from clairvoyance? The term "telepathy" was originally used by F. W. H. Myers, who, in the nineteenth century, founded the Society for Psychical Research in London.

When Myers used his expression, it meant a communication from one mind to another without the use of any of the five senses. When he coined the word "telepathy," he distinguished "mental" telepathy from "clairvoyant" telepathy. Mental telepathy consisted of thoughts transferred from one mind to the other. Clairvoyant telepathy was "seeing" an action that was going on simultaneously between one person and another. The following examples will demonstrate the difference between telepathy and clairvoyance.

You and I are seated at a table across from each other. On the table is a deck of cards. You select a card—and you see it is the king of hearts, but you do not tell me this. You then ask me if I know what the card is, and I say it is the king of hearts.
This is telepathy.

You and I are seated at the same table, still across from each other. On the table is a deck of cards. You select a card, *but this time you do not look at it.* The card remains face down on the table. You then ask me if I know what the card is, and I say it is the king of hearts.
This is clairvoyance.

While clairvoyance can include telepathy, telepathy cannot include clairvoyance.

Let's look at another personal experience to get a better idea of how telepathy works. Keith Garber, a national bridge champion who also works in data communications, tells of a telepathic experience he had:

"I had met a very interesting woman companion one Sunday, and had an appointment to meet her at 8:00 the Monday evening following. As I approached my home on the afternoon before our date, I had a very strong urge to buy her a plant. I saw a florist shop in front of me and started to go in, but upon checking my wallet, found I only had $3, which would not be enough money, so I abandoned the idea. That day was very hectic in my office and I had no time to get to a bank. That evening, en route to meet my friend, I again was seized with the idea that I wanted to buy her a plant. As I parked my car and got out, I saw in front of me another florist shop. However, it was 7:30 P.M. and it was closed. In any event, I still only had the same $3, since I had been unable to cash a check yet. At that point, I had a flash through my mind that my friend had gotten me a gift. I took out my pen, looked for a piece of paper to write on, and scribbled a note to this effect: 'Thank you for the gift. I would have reciprocated, but found I only had $3 on me.'

"I then went to meet my friend. As we entered the car, she gave me a small bag, which I started to put in the back seat of the car. 'No,' she said, 'that's for you.' Upon opening it, I found it was a plant. I then gave her the scribbled note thanking her, which rather astonished her."

This is a fine example of telepathy. Keith was receiving his friend's thoughts about wanting to buy him a gift. He felt this so strongly that he wrote a note of apology in advance, indicating why he could not reciprocate.

For another example, Mr. Leslie Price, Member of the Council of the British Society for Psychical Research, was visiting in the United States and told of this incident: "On Saturday, October 30, 1976, as I arrived at the American Society for Psychical Research, a staff member handed me a letter from George Meek, the healing researcher. I had hoped to meet George Meek while I was in the United States on this trip, but, unfortunately, Mr. Meek was scheduled to be in the Middle East while I was in the United States. On Monday, the first of November, as I was walking through New York on my way to an appointment at a publisher, I passed the Roosevelt Hotel and I saw standing there, greatly to my surprise, Mr. George Meek! Thus, although we had assumed that it would not be possible to meet in New York, a meeting had taken place by the most unlikely of coincidences. Mr. Meek was about to board a bus to take him to the airport to catch the plane to the Middle East. As a consequence of our meeting, we were able to exchange useful information on developments in the psychic field."

I asked Leslie if the possibility existed that either he or George Meek, or both, may have felt pangs that this meeting could not take place and therefore a telepathic communication occurred which enabled them to meet. Leslie replied, "Possibly, because although I was proceeding through New York to a definite destination, obviously in my choice of which blocks to walk along, there was a certain element of randomness." When I inquired if Leslie knew that Mr. Meek was staying at the Roosevelt, he replied that not only did he not know which hotel he was at, but "I was most surprised to see George Meek in New York!"

Are there certain conditions that foster telepathy more than others? According to experts in the field, such as D. Scott Rogo, David Hammond, and Eileen Garrett, telepathy occurs most frequently under emotional or stress situations. The eminent parapsychologist Raynor C. Johnson states, "Some of the most interesting and convincing examples of telepathy occur in everyday life. They are of no evidential value to anyone except the immediate experiencer, but where they are of frequent occurrence to a person, they leave little room for doubt."[3] Further to the point, Mrs. Eileen J. Garrett, the famous medium and psychic healer, states in her classic work, *Telepathy*: ". . . when I stress at this point that in my opinion telepa-

3. Johnson, *Psychical Research*, pp. 9, 10.

thy presupposes a use of the emotions, I mean exactly what I say. I believe that true telepathic communication can only be obtained through emotional transmission and reception. Out of such emotional experiences can later be developed an intellectual concept, but I am convinced that telepathy cannot be successfully produced by a purely mental and laboratory approach."

An example of how emotional transmission and reception might work is the following experience: During a further conversation in a meeting with Leslie Price during his visit to the United States, the name of Dr. Lawrence LeShan, the noted parapsychologist, arose. My husband and I had not seen Larry for a number of years. As it happened, the previous week I had written Dr. LeShan a letter to ask if he would read the manuscript of my book before publication. I had sent the letter to his office. It was returned, indicating he was no longer at that address. I then decided to send the letter to his home address "Certified Mail—return receipt requested," which guarantees the sender that the letter did indeed arrive at its destination. However, I had not received the return receipt back and the post office could find no record that a delivery had been made. Since Larry had a new, unlisted telephone, which I did not know, I could not call.

My husband, Leslie and I had finished lunch, and were strolling in Central Park, when lo and behold there appeared Larry LeShan and his wife standing in front of us. This meeting gave me the opportunity to ask Larry personally if he would read the manuscript, which he agreed to do.

This is an instance of how stress plays a role in telepathy. Since I was very concerned that the book accurately reflect my early meetings with Dr. LeShan, and since I was equally concerned that the letter I sent might not have reached him, this may have been a factor in a telepathic communication. I do not see the meeting as merely coincidence.

However, because I am a layperson and wished a professional opinion, I wrote to Ruby Yeatman who had this to say about the above events: "I found the accounts you gave of the incidents which happened to Leslie and George Meek, and to you, Leslie and Dr. LeShan most intriguing. My feeling, for what it is worth, is that YOU, Katy, being engaged upon what will be an important book on psychic work and personalities, are subconsciously pushed towards those people and events which are of use, or likely to be of use, in the fulfillment of your work as a whole, and more than that which will have further import and use in the future. I agree that subconsciously, or by telepathic rapport, Leslie and George Meek were drawn into one another's orbit and to a place where they could meet, and this also would apply to your meeting with Dr. LeShan. I think you, rather than Leslie, act as it were as the catalyst, although I freely admit both the incidents could be rationally explained by telepathic contact, or equally by co-incidence; but I myself lean to the less acceptable explanation, for most people of influence from the Unseen. You will perhaps smile, but there is the power of the soul and the superconscious, if you like. The soul of a person has tremendous power. I DO feel that your incidents *are* meaningful."

For a dramatic telepathic communication that was received under an emotional or crisis situation, we can cite the following quote from David Hammond: "A husband wakes in the middle of the night, shakes his wife and tells her he has a feeling that something dreadful has happened to their son. Two hours later, they receive a call from the police informing them that the boy has been in a serious accident."[4] Hammond relates this experience in connection with his interview with Stanley Krippner, chief of the Dream Laboratory at Maimonides Hospital, Brooklyn, New York. Hammond considered it a telepathic dream and stated that telepathy generally occurs in dramatically emotional situations between two people.

Eileen Garrett propounded an interesting and unique hypothesis that telepathy was man's lost sixth sense. She strongly felt that primitive man, in his evolution, made extensive use of telepathy as his prime means of communication. Long before speech had evolved, and certainly before the first attempts at writing had occurred, man used transmission of thoughts and impressions to others of his tribe—telepathy—as his prime means of communication. She asserted that gradually, as man developed both speech and writing, his instinctive method of communication was forgotten and, finally, disappeared from the area of human accomplishments. Mrs. Garrett went on to say that telepathic power remained in man in a backward, if not latent, state. She was convinced that every person is born with this, that it is suppressed by modern society, but that it is a faculty that modern man must relearn if he is to become one with his world—his universe.

What, if any, are the practical uses of telepathy? If by practical we mean "get-rich-quick schemes" such as playing horses or the stock market, or knowing what lottery ticket to buy, etc., telepathy or any of the forms of ESP will be of little help. If by practical we mean telepathic communication between friends or relatives in the times of emotional crisis or danger, telepathy has played and will undoubtedly continue to play a significantly useful role.

However, telepathy's greatest use may be in man's expanding development of the "thinking" faculty—to help him understand the oneness of the universe. Man need no longer think of himself as a small helpless individual, lost in a universal void—but, rather, as a link in a creative and thinking process that knew no beginning and knows no end.

Telepathy could be the principal means of communication between people in the future. Once it has been developed and refined into the "sixth" sense, as envisaged by Eileen Garrett, telepathy will be faster, surer, and more accurate than letters, telegrams, telephone calls, and even television. After all, there is nothing faster or more accurate than instant thought transference.

In the beginning of this book, I described my first chance meeting with Eileen Garrett in the lobby of my apartment house. Some years later, Eileen was residing both in France and in Florida. Although we had kept

4. Hammond, *The Search for Psychic Power*, p. 151.

in touch, we had not seen each other for a long time. Eileen was very ill by then, but nonetheless we arranged a time to meet in New York in the month of March. I had been recuperating from a fractured ankle, and on the morning of our scheduled meeting, I arose to find snow and ice on the ground. Inasmuch as my accident with the ankle had occurred on ice, I was fearful of the icy conditions of the streets, and called to say I could not meet her on that day. A few weeks later—just as years earlier I had felt a strong urge to go to the lobby of my building, where I was to first meet Eileen Garrett—so did I now have a similar compulsion to go immediately to that same lobby. Standing before me as I opened the elevator door was Eileen, accompanied by a nurse. She was ill . . . dying I thought . . . and since she was to depart for France soon, we kissed goodbye.

Eileen never returned to America, and died some months later in her beloved France. I would challenge anyone who would deny that the initial meeting of and the ultimate farewell between Eileen Garrett and Katy Donnelly in the lobby of an apartment house didn't have emotional impact.

And *that* is what telepathy is all about.

7

Precognition

A friend of mine, Elizabeth Cornelis, had a problem in her place of employment. She tells of subsequent events:

"It was the practice of the company I worked for to give increases in salary on a semi-annual basis. On one of these anniversaries, I learned that I had been the only one among the clerical staff to be an exception to this practice. Deep hurt settled within me. Upon learning of my depressed state of mind, Katy telephoned and we made arrangements to meet. She offered considerable comfort, dried my tears, and proceeded to tell me about a change for me that would occur within the very near future. Thinking it a ruse to console me, I listened attentively but had my doubts.

"Katy said I would soon be transferred to another department on another floor, at the farthest end of the building, far removed from where I was located at the time. She further stated that a promotion, a change in title, and a sizable increment would be forthcoming.

"Within a month's time or shortly thereafter, I was offered a transfer into another department which was located on another floor and, indeed, at the farthest end of the building! A promotion and change of title did occur and since that time the increments have been many."

And on another occasion:

The late Maurice Woodruff, the famous English clairvoyant, was in New York for a television series dealing with ESP. I had been invited by the producer, Paul Alter, to attend one of the evening programs and was told I would have a visit with Maurice after the program. During our meeting after the show, Maurice told me I must hurry home quickly because my husband would be taken ill with a kidney stone problem and that we would have to call a doctor in the middle of the night.

Rather than continue the visit with Maurice, I immediately took my leave and hurried home. When I arrived, my husband complained of a backache, but there did not seem to be severe stress, and we went to bed. Some hours later, in the middle of the night, he was in agonizing pain and we called an emergency doctor to pay a house call. Upon examining my husband, the doctor diagnosed the pain as a symptom of a passing kidney stone. He gave my husband an injection of morphine and advised him to see his family doctor in the morning. The next morning, our doctor agreed that it indeed was a kidney stone and gave my husband a relaxant. The stone passed that afternoon. Maurice Woodruff's vision had been correct.

What precisely is precognition? "Cognition" is probably best defined as the capability of knowing. "Precognition," therefore, is the ability of knowing beforehand. If an individual has knowledge about an event that will take place in the future—be it one hour, one day, one week, or longer—and *there is no available information that could be used to explain the event*, such knowledge is precognition.

Now that we are aware of what precognition is, let's also learn what precognition is not:

You dream of receiving a letter from a person who has not written you for some time. Two days later the letter arrives. This is probably an example of telepathy between you and the writer or an example of clairvoyance—you "see" the letter already in existence. It is *not* precognition.

How does precognition differ from telepathy or clairvoyance? Precognition is a process similar to both telepathy and clairvoyance, only occurring under different time circumstances. In many instances, it is difficult to distinguish between these three forms of ESP. For example: You receive an impression of the death of a friend, and later learn that the death did occur on the same day you received the thought. Is it a clairvoyant impression of a distant occurrence, or is it telepathy from either the individual involved or someone who witnessed the event, or is it precognitive if the death occurred an hour or so later than the time you received the impression?

We should, therefore, consider all facets of ESP—regardless of the forms they take—as a whole, each faculty being just another manifestation of the same process.

One morning my husband told me he had to fly to Texas on business for a week and suggested I accompany him. While packing our suitcase, I suddenly got the impression that our luggage might be lost, and Mexico appeared very prominently in the impression I was receiving. My husband's business associate, Don, was also going on the trip.

I told my husband that if he had any important materials needed for his business in Houston not to pack them in the suitcase but to carry them on board. I was afraid the luggage would be lost.

Prior to our departure to the airport, Don called to say he would have to take a later plane and would meet us in Texas. I asked my husband to tell Don to also take aboard any essential materials. However, because Don was a business associate, my husband felt embarrassed and apprehensive about injecting ESP into their discussion and decided not to do so.

When my husband and I arrived at the airport, our luggage was taken from us, but the porter failed to give us any baggage receipts. I felt uneasy about it and suggested we contact the baggage captain to make sure our luggage was headed for the Houston flight. When the baggage was not found among the other luggage, I asked that we check the baggage area of the next scheduled flight to Mexico. When we did, there was our luggage, *almost* en route to Mexico.

Later that evening, Don took his scheduled flight to Houston. However, his luggage did not accompany him—it went to Mexico!

This is an instance where precognition can be of importance. Because my husband had been alerted to my precognitive impression, he brought all the necessary business forms aboard with him. Unbeknownst to me, he also brought extra business materials for Don—"to play it safe." He later told me that if he had not brought the extra materials, the business project would have been aborted, since Don had packed everything into his luggage rather than bringing it aboard.

In this chapter we will present the views of several authorities in the field, among whom is Ruby Yeatman, who feels that knowing the future gives you the information and the power to change it. The above incident of the luggage to Mexico is an example of how the future can be changed.

When is precognition most likely to happen? Experiments by researchers seem to indicate that precognition takes place about two-thirds of the time during sleep and about one-third of the time while awake.

Examples of precognitive dreams have occurred throughout history: There is the biblical account of Joseph's interpretation of the Pharaoh's dream of "seven fat years and seven lean years"; one can also cite the precognitive dream of Emperor Augustus Caesar, who foresaw the birth of Christ and his being a "King of Peace." Saint Catherine of Siena in the fourteenth century had a precognitive dream that Pope Gregory XI, who was then residing in Avignon, France, would bring the Papacy back to Rome. This was to occur two years later. Considering that the Popes had been out of Rome and residing in France for the past hundred years, Saint Catherine's dream was indeed prophetic. And there was Abraham Lincoln's dream of his own assassination, to cite but a few.

A less dramatic but more current precognitive dream is that told by Andrew Bato, Director of Research at a major advertising company in New York:

"My wife and I were on the tail end of our honeymoon in Bermuda. Rather than returning on a scheduled flight, we decided to try to get a cabin on the sailing of the *Queen of Bermuda.* I telephoned the Furness Line to request space, but the sailing was sold out. Although I asked to be put on the waiting list, they held out little hope.

"Two nights before the ship was due to sail, I dreamed that the phone in our hotel room was ringing. Still in the dream I answered the phone but could hear nothing. Since the only call we would be likely to receive would be from the Furness Line, I had the feeling they were trying to reach us to tell us a cabin was available.

"The dream came early in the night, so I went back to sleep. Around 9 A.M., when I was awake, the phone actually rang. I answered it and was greeted by complete and utter silence. I hung up, thinking that it was a mistake on the operator's part, and in any event there seemed to be nothing I could do right away, since I had not yet been up to shave and dress. Then I hit upon the idea of picking up the phone, waiting briefly, and telling the operator that I could not hear her but that if she could hear me, she should make the phone ring three times after I hung up. I hung up, and almost instantly, the three rings came, confirming that the phone was out of order. I acknowledged them with thanks, threw on some clothes, and went down to the lobby to call the Furness Line on a coin telephone.

" 'Yes, Mr. Bato, we have been trying to reach you. We have an inside stateroom for you.' Naturally I accepted.

"Considering the combination of having the receiving but not the transmitting end of a hotel room telephone go dead *and* dreaming about it before it happened *and* a height-of-season cancellation on a fully booked ship, the odds against this three-way parlay must be impressive, to say the least."

Are certain conditions necessary to precognition? Precognition occurs most frequently under conditions of powerful emotional crisis—war, disaster, separation, death, accident, serious illness. Under such circumstances the mind comes under great stress and needs the precognitive outlet to act as a form of calming sedation. Precognition is also likely to occur between people who are very emotionally attached and who experience some great crisis where they need each other's aid.

Precognition—and other forms of ESP—manifests itself especially in times of war, when we experience a time of great crisis or disaster, coupled with long periods of separation from emotionally bound individuals and loved ones.

In Eileen Garrett's book *Beyond The Five Senses*, there is a chapter written by Hans Bender, entitled "Provisions of Disaster." Professor Bender's short introduction eloquently conveys the effect war plays in the increase of precognition and the other talents of ESP:

"War seems to bring with it an increase in the occurrence of paranormal phenomena, as fears and tensions batter against separation in time and space. An analysis of such experiences was undertaken in Germany by the Freiburg Institute, which found no oracular forecast of war, but case upon case of personal forewarning expressed in precognition, true dream, second sight, and apparition. Only when it is related to one's personal destiny does the collective fate of mankind seem involuntarily now and then to light up in mysterious fragments."[1]

Further to this point, Professor Bender adds: "Misfortune, separation, sickness, danger to life and limb, loss of property—these too motivate telepathic, clairvoyant, and precognitive impressions far more frequently than do feelings of joy or indifference."[2]

I should like now to give you the benefit of some of the answers from

1. Garrett, *Beyond the Five Senses*, p. 136.
2. Ibid., p. 136.

Ruby Yeatman to questions regarding precognition and knowing the future:

What is precognition and when did it begin? "Perception, knowledge, understanding arrived at independently of the reason or by any known process of acquisition. It has, I imagine, always been a property of the human being, at any rate of civilised man—by civilised I mean once he had emerged from his prehistoric state. All through the Bible instances of precognition occur."

How would one know if one had precognition? "It is recognised by the individual who has it by the fact that it is 'other' than normal cognition of objects and knowledge; its impact is often sudden and carries forceful conviction.

How reliable are precognitive impressions and of what use are they? "There are many recorded instances of reliable precognitive impressions which may be read in the proceedings and journals of the Society for Psychical Research, in very many books written by men and women of integrity and distinction, such as those by Sir William Barrett, F. W. H. Myers, Professor Richet and dozens of others. . . . The precognitive faculty has also been of great use in diagnosis in regard to health and disease."

Why does so much trivia seem to be involved in precognition? "Trivia and triviality occur in all forms of psychic sensitivity, possibly because psychic gifts, being an extension of the five physical senses, enable the individual to pick up, or sense, all kinds of 'bits and pieces' not necessarily of any particular importance."

Do most people want to know the future? "A difficult question to answer for some people would declare that to know the future (prevision, precognition and premonition) can be very valuable and helpful. There is in many people a keen desire to learn something of what may be in store for them, hence the attraction (to some extent) of fortunetellers, good, bad and indifferent. Others prefer not to know anything of the future in any of its aspects and some due to religious belief consider it to be wrong to pry into the unknown. It is a matter for individual judgment."

Can anything be changed by knowing the future? How can visions of disasters prevent them? "One could go about changing the future by using common sense. . . . The vision alone could not prevent a disaster; it is the action taken either by the individual to whom the vision is vouchsafed, or by the person to whom the vision applies, which might result in disaster being prevented. A friend of mine, who was a gifted clairvoyant, was to travel with a friend to the North of England. On the platform, just before the train was due to leave, she clairvoyantly saw a terrible accident happening to the train. She forcibly prevented her friend from getting into the carriage and the train left without them. Later they learnt that there had been a terrible accident with great loss of life: the carriage in which they would have been sitting was wrecked. . . . We have the power to make choices within certain boundaries. . . . I would say that we have free will within the limits of His eternal laws."

What is the difference between precognition and premonition? Precognition, as previously defined, is the seeing or knowing of a future event before it actually happens. Premonition, on the other hand, is a less precise vision, but one that many times forebodes disaster.

William Oliver Stevens tells of a premonition, or "hunch," of a famous surgeon during World War II:

"The popular name for premonition is 'hunch,' meaning a vague uneasy feeling that something is wrong with a loved one or that something needs to be done. This is the word used by Dr. Gordon Seagrave, the 'Burma Surgeon,' in telling of an utterly unreasonable thing that he felt compelled to do one day during the late war. (*Burma Surgeon Returns*, p. 132). He writes:

Early on the morning of May 17, 1944, I was tossing sleeplessly on my bed, wishing it were time to get up. . . . One of those incredible hunches hit me. Something was cooking. I hustled the boys out of bed and ordered them to evacuate all our remaining patients to the Chinese Regimental Hospital. While they emptied the wards, our few Chinese, our Burmese boys and I pulled the tents down and rolled them up. When the trucks returned, we loaded them with equipment for a surgical hospital. Everyone thought the Old Man had gone mad."[3]

Even though it seemed like a crazy thing to do at the time, Seagrave later received unexpected orders to evacuate his area as quickly as possible because of impending enemy action. The premonition he received was so strong that he acted on it, even though it was contrary to every reasonable expectation.

An experience of my own, although bordering on precognition, probably falls into the category of premonition:

On November 28, 1967, while standing in a subway station, my legs began to wobble and then shake. I thought it must be the tremor of the platform, but no trains were in sight which might have caused this shaking sensation. Again, I felt the shaking and "saw" that an earthquake had split the ground. Two large letters "DD" loomed in front of me, and the Roman numeral I appeared in front of the name of the subway station at 74th Street. In relating the incident to my husband when I arrived home, I told him I felt that in a matter of days there would be some relationship to the name of the subway station "74th Street." My husband asked if perhaps the D stood for "Big D" because I had been born in Dallas. I replied, "No, it wasn't Dallas; it appeared more like Denver, or Denber." My husband said it couldn't be Denver, because no earthquakes occur there.

Two days later, a television news broadcaster announced the story of an

3. William Oliver Stevens, *Psychics and Common Sense: An Introduction to the Study of Psychic Phenomena* (New York: E. P. Dutton Co., 1953), p. 99.

earthquake in Debar, Yugoslavia. The newspaper story carried by the *New York Times* stated 174 people were injured, which bore out the relationship of the subway station of 74th Street, preceded by the numeral I. The double D (DD) still puzzled me, but the answer was forthcoming when shortly thereafter my husband read an article in the *Wall Street Journal* with the headline "Man-Made Earthquakes In Denver" which told of underground experiments by the Army.

Why are accurate psychic predictions of events sometimes inaccurate in timing? Timing in some instances seems to be amiss. Even though a prediction may be right, the timing may be off.

In an interview with Judith Richardson Haimes, a well-known psychic who not only reads the aura but assists in helping as an investigative aid to police in solving crime, she tells of the timing problem to the psychic:

"Ninety-five percent of my mistakes are in my timing. I will explain to you in layman's terms why.

"If you saw a man standing against a blue wall and he was wearing a blue suit, and there was nothing but the man and the wall, and someone said to you, 'how tall is he,' you could not tell if he was 5'6" or 6'5". You have nothing to compare it to. Just as in a photograph, if you only saw a man and a blank wall, you could not determine his height. Timing, such as we know it here on this plane in this dimension, is different than what you are seeing."

Similarly, Judith asserts that mistakes are made by psychics because there is no standard or time band with which to compare what the psychics "see."

In other words, if there was a gauge of 5 feet, 6 feet, or 7 feet on the wall which Judith speaks of above, then you could judge the height of the man. And, such a gauge would also serve in the same manner to provide an indicator in judging the time element in psychic predictions.

At this point, let's turn to Eileen Garrett's universal philosophy about extrasensory perception. In her book *Many Voices* she tells of her experiences with precognition:

"Precognition has been a common occurrence with me all my life, but I have had to think of some hypothesis that might make it more intelligible to myself. Since I truly believe that eternity is here and now and that all aspects of the self are contained within the absolute, I do not regard precognition as being very different from the other patterns contained within the mind. . . . We have access to its infinite corridors of experience, finding our way at times into a new room which we think of as the future, when in actuality that room *has always been.* It is coming into existence only as we perceive it, but we have had time along the way to 'make friends' with many aspects of the collective unconscious flow of energy that we describe as mind."

Is there any danger in knowing the future? A real danger that lies in precognition is allowing fear to rule us. I remember an instance that occurred many years ago when Romola Nijinsky, wife of the famous dancer Vaslav Nijinsky, was visiting in our home with friends. Romola had just flown in from Europe. During the course of the conversation, Romola told how she had been upset during the flight to New York, because at one point it seemed that the plane might have to land in Paris. The reason for her great alarm was that a medium had told her she would die in Paris. This was a very real fear for Romola, and she suffered great distress at the possibility of the plane landing in Paris.

Now, these many years later, she has developed an interesting philosophy concerning Paris and in a recent letter wrote, "Now, I am just going in January to Paris, to settle there for good. . . . I do not fear any more to be in Paris, as I became after many very interesting events a *fatalist*. . . . I am convinced now that at the time of our birth already the events of our life and the time of our death is decided."

Should one attempt to guide one's life through precognitive or other ESP information? Lawrence LeShan presents the following view:

"Planning and acting on the basis of paranormally acquired information is just plain kookiness at this stage of our knowledge of the paranormal. This is a viewpoint I learned from Eileen Garrett, who was probably the most talented and most widely and carefully studied acquirer of paranormal information of our time. (The technical term for a person with a great deal of ability in this area is a 'sensitive.') Mrs. Garrett believed that one never acted on the basis of information acquired through paranormal means, only on the information acquired by normal means. She made one exception to this rule. If you have never had any particularly strong fear of flying and are about to get on an airplane and feel a very strong, unusual anxiety about going on this particular plane, delay your flight to a later one. This response was the only exception to her rule."[4]

Was precognition ever within the range of the "normal" senses or was it always the province of the gifted few? It would be hard to disagree with Eileen Garrett's thesis that precognition is another one of the ESP faculties that primitive man possessed. His cave painting, which depicts the hunt and the kill of animals that would provide his food, would appear to have a twofold message. One, the belief that by painting the animals being hunted and being killed, man possessed the power to bring this about. The second and more subtle message was that the painter possibly knew in advance through precognitive thought which of the various beasts would appear and where the animals would appear, and painted these pictures of successful future hunts.

It might be argued that primitive man, being so close to the animal state, may have been able to communicate telepathically with the animals themselves. On the other hand, perhaps it was not man but rather the animals who communicated telepathically. Perhaps the animals never lost this faculty.

The renowned mystic and psychic healer Olga Worrall claims that animals flock to her because they sense she is a healer. Perhaps they also sense her other psychic powers.

4. LeShan, *How to Meditate*, p. 51.

Unfortunately for man, the precognitive faculty of communication was forgotten and lost for many thousands of years. It would appear occasionally in historical time, but except in classical Greece and Rome, it never was given much credence. In fact, in medieval Christian countries, precognition was considered the work of demons, devils, and witches. Fortunately, today, this so-called lost faculty is being retrained. It undoubtedly will play a greater role in man's life in the future. Where precognition and the other forms of ESP will lead us is anyone's guess. We can only hope that this "bonus" for mankind will be harnessed for our benefit and not our destruction.

Is precognition always gloom and doom?

Definitely not, although, as we have discussed, crisis situations seem to act as catalysts in bringing about precognitive visions. However, it is also possible to give love, help, peace of mind, comfort, and solace in precognitive thoughts, as was the case in the following experience related by engineering manager Frank Palermo, who, some time prior to the following events, had discussed a particular problem with me:

"My wife and I were contemplating a move from New York to New Jersey, but were apprehensive about it. I met Katy one day and told her of our difficulty in selecting a home which would be suitable for our needs.

"Katy immediately responded, 'Frank, you will know the house when you discover that it is a house that has been filled with love.' I asked her if she could be more explicit. 'Someone will tell you that it was a house filled with love and that is the reason it will be sold to you.'

"This conversation was for the most part forgotten until one day I was taken to see the outside of a house which was to be placed on the market the following Saturday. Trying not to show my enthusiasm, I admitted a certain mild interest to the real estate saleswoman and arranged for the house to be shown to my wife.

"That weekend we looked at the house, and while there spoke with the owner, a recent widow. She indicated that she hated to sell the house and move, but could not bear the thought of living alone in the house since her husband's death, because until then 'it was a house that has been filled with love.' She said she wanted to be sure that the house went to a couple with 'love in their home.'

"We bought the house, needless to say, moved in, and to this day can feel the warmth, love, and charm transmitted."

Is there someone to whom you can turn if you have a premonition and want to see if it is accurate? If you believe you have received a warning of disaster, or if you wish to research the area of premonitions, you can contact the Central Premonitions Registry (P.O. Box 482, Times Square Station, New York, New York 10031). In the May-June 1976 issue of the *Parapsychology Review*, Robert Nelson, Director of the Registry explains: "Each first-time writer receives a standard-response letter explaining the procedures for filing premonitions and instructions as to monitoring dreams for possibly psi-induced material. (Psi is merely a simplified abbreviation used by parapsychologists in referring to psychic phenomena.)

Upon request photo-copies of predictions date-stamped 'Registered C.P.R.' are sent to the participants. Anyone who shows psi-talent by achieving a 'hit,' a close correspondence between a registered event and subsequent actual occurrence, or who relates highly detailed and significant past precognitive experiences, is sent a Psi Profile Questionnaire." Mr. Nelson indicates that many letters received at the Registry pertain to inquiries by persons seeking aid in finding missing relatives, lost possessions, etc. However, most of those who write are people who feel they may have had a premonition or precognitive dream, thought, or vision and are very happy to know that their predictions or premonitions are going to be taken seriously. Since its inception, the Registry has been mentioned in more than 300 newspapers in the United States, Canada, and Europe. Contributors from more than twenty foreign countries and thousands of people from every state have written to the Registry, with several hundred submitting between three and fifty letters yearly.

Several other psychical societies have their own premonitions bureau, such as the Toronto Society for Psychical Research in Canada, and the Society for Psychic Research in Beverly Hills, California.

CHAPTER
8

Clairvoyance

In the eighteenth century, while residing in Gothenburg, Emanuel Sweden-borg, the Swedish philosopher and scientist, "saw" and very accurately described a fire ravaging Stockholm some 300 miles away. *Two days later*, news of the conflagration reached Gothenburg. The news carried a description of the fire. It was similar on all counts to the description given by Swedenborg!

In her book *Many Voices*, Eileen Garrett describes her meeting and subsequent marriage in 1915 to a "boyish young man." The marriage was short-lived:

"Within a month he was dead. Dining with some friends at the Savoy Hotel in London one evening, I had clairvoyantly seen my young husband blown up with two or three other people. I appeared to be caught by the smoke and explosion within a sea of sound, even to be a part of the dread experience. I became ill and begged to be excused. A few days later, I was advised by the War Office that he was among the missing. His brother officers later wrote that he had gone on a wire-cutting expedition and never returned. Years later I saw his name on the Menis Gate Memorial at Ypres [Belgium]. Only I knew the manner in which he had died."

Elizabeth Cornelis recounts a less dramatic but more mundane clairvoyant experience we shared some time back:

"I recall a most astonishing occasion when I had misplaced a sum of money which was to be deposited in the bank, but instead had been carelessly left on a ledge in the kitchen. The deposit had to be postponed —the kitchen ceiling collapsed! What a mess! In haste, I transferred all kitchen paraphernalia to the small bedroom and patiently waited for repairs. After the furor had subsided, I was in a complete frenzy trying to remember where I had secreted the money. A search of hiding places was to no avail. It was during these hectic moments that Katy called. No sooner had I mentioned my dilemma when she told me to look in the small bedroom on the coffee table for a book which was hidden under something. There I would find the money, she said, which would be sticking out of the book just a little.

"Without hesitation, I flew into the bedroom, but could not find such a book, and Katy and I terminated our conversation. I went back into the bedroom once more, dug into the maze of assorted kitchenware, and uncovered a cookbook which contained the money. Oh, yes—it was sticking out of the book all right—just a little!"

However, because I am a layperson, I sought a professional opinion from Ruby Yeatman, former principal of the College of Psychic Studies in London. In reply to my question as to what this experience might be called, Ruby replied: "Now about your experience when you were able to tell your friend exactly where she would find the misplaced money, in my opinion this is genuine clairvoyance and not telepathy."

And from bank executive John Raffa comes this account:

"Upon returning to my office I learned from my secretary that Katy had called and had asked that I be given a message to please have my blood checked. As it happened, I had a physical examination scheduled shortly thereafter. Many tests, including one of the blood, were taken. When the results returned, I had a discussion with the doctor. He told me the blood test revealed that I had Thalassemia Minor—sometimes known as Mediterranean anemia.

"He told me my records indicated that this had appeared the previous year in my physical examination. I told the doctor that I had *not* been informed of this last year and that this was the first time I had heard about it. He was quite surprised and thought the laboratory would have sent the results to me. Inadvertently, it appeared my records had been filed away, without any notification to me about the results of the blood test.

"I was not aware that the condition existed; this doctor was not the doctor who received the previous year's results; the doctor this year had not been aware that I had not received the previous year's test results. There is no way Katy could have known from me or the doctors that this condition existed.

"Now, in being aware of it, the problem can be dealt with properly through medical guidance."

What is clairvoyance? The term "clairvoyance" comes from the French; translated literally, it means a "clear seeing."

David Hammond, author of *The Search for Psychic Power*, defines clairvoyance as "the awareness of an object or an objective event not obtained through the use of the other senses, and the perception is simultaneous with the event."[1]

Similarly, Dr. Raynor C. Johnson, in his book *Psychical Research*, explains, "The term clairvoyance . . . refers to the mind's power of acquiring knowledge of physical objects or events (as distinct from mental ones) without the use of any of the recognised channels of sense."[2]

1. Hammond, *The Search for Psychic Power*, pp. 9–10.
2. Johnson, *Psychical Research*, p. 9.

What is the difference between clairvoyance, telepathy, and precognition? One of the most important things to remember about clairvoyance is that information concerning an ongoing object or event is seen from a distance and is not received mentally. This is the principal distinction between telepathy—information being received mentally, as a thought—and clairvoyance—information being received through some form of "sight," as if a scene were being viewed.

However, clairvoyance and precognition are very similar processes only occurring under different circumstances. Time is the determining factor. If you receive an impression of an accident at the time such an accident does occur, you are probably experiencing a clairvoyant event. However, if the accident does not occur until several days or weeks later, that would probably be a precognitive event.

The following is an example of a clairvoyant, rather than a precognitive, experience:

One afternoon, I was in a taxi on my way to an appointment with Dr. Lawrence LeShan at the Union Theological Seminary in New York when I suddenly "saw" Larry sitting in his office, and flames surrounding the area in which his office building was situated. I felt the fire was much too close to Larry and I was concerned for his well-being. As the taxi approached Larry's office building, firemen were trying to contain the flames that were shooting out of the seminary building across the street. Fortunately, neither Larry nor his office were harmed.

What is a clairvoyant "picture" like? "There are various types of clairvoyant experiences," wrote Eileen Garrett in *Adventures in the Supernatural.* "Not all of them are dependent on the flow of imagery, but may occur in the unaccountable appearance of a strange picture in which one sees through and beyond barriers that would completely balk our ordinary sensory vision. A road may wind among hills for any distance. One sees the hills and as the road reaches away, perspective operates and its farther dimensions diminish, as they would diminish to our sight or in any picture. Nevertheless, at the same time, one sees the entire road completely, regardless of the intervening hills, and its farther reaches are as meticulously discernible as the areas that lie close to the spot from which one is seeing. Each rut and stone is individually seen and can be described with precision. The leaves of trees and the blades of grass are countable throughout the landscape."

In a recent informal discussion, Professor W. H. C. Tenhaeff, Director of the Parapsychological Institute of the State University of Utrecht, Holland, explained how difficult it is for many tested sensitives to describe what they "see," "hear," "feel," "experience," etc.

Not only is it difficult to discern these types of sensations, but sensitives seem to have even greater difficulty in providing descriptions of the way in which they "see," "hear," etc. Professor Tenhaeff explained that in many instances this is due to the sensitives' inability to express themselves, and also to their unfamiliarity with technical psychological terms. The sensitives, according to Professor Tenhaeff, have a graphic as well as a nongraphic knowing:

"With the non-graphic knowing we have apparently to do with knowledge forcing itself upon them, with ideas (notions) pressing themselves upon them, with a 'knowing' attended by an evidence-consciousness which appears capable of showing various degrees of strength. The testee, for instance, 'knows' that the inductor (a fingerprint in this case) has something to do with a girl who 'is not quite normal,' who had an abortion, was assaulted, and tried to take her own life.

"This 'knowing' seems to pass very easily into a 'seeing,' a 'hearing,' and a 'feeling.' The testee then suddenly 'sees' the person about whom he 'knew' certain things, with . . . clearness before him. If we question the testee . . . we find that [his] pictures are sometimes vague and then again uncommonly sharp.

"It appears that their pictures are sometimes two-dimensional and then again three-dimensional. A testee told me that whenever he 'saw' something in three dimensions, he 'knew' that what he saw really existed. If he 'saw' something in two dimensions, he had to allow for the possibility of undergoing a telepathic influence from the side of a consultant. It should be stressed that not all the testees make a similar distinction between two- and three-dimensional pictures."[3]

Professor Tenhaeff goes on to relate that the "pictures" that appear to the sensitive are alternately dynamic and static, with some indicating "a film passing at a great speed before their mind's eye of which they can 'keep' (remember) only a few fragments. . . . All pictures are not equally clear either." When inquiring of a famous sensitive, Mrs. Akkeringa, if she could "stop" this film, he was told that it was impossible for her to do so. "She was unable to influence the speed through her will. Some other paragnosts (sensitives) made similar remarks."

When questioning testees with respect to the color aspect of their "pictures," it was found that plain pictures were mentioned as well as colored ones, with many sensitives seeing both. "This is for instance the case with Mr. G. Croiset. He says that he usually 'sees' in black-and-white. But if it is necessary . . . (e.g., in the case of loss), things appear to him in colours as they really are. In a consultation by telephone, for example, the picture of a lighthouse with four windows appeared to him. Under one of the windows he 'saw' two yellow stains, caused by rust. On verification the picture proved to be correct."

Is there historical evidence to substantiate the claims of clairvoyants? Historically, clairvoyance has been an accepted phenomenon since early times. Some of its most ardent supporters belonged to the medical profession. Hippocrates believed that bodily illnesses could be diagnosed by the clairvoyant dreams of the patients themselves.

A famous medical work, *On Regimen*, written in the fourth century, makes mention of "medical clairvoyance." It stated that during sleep, the soul surveys the internal structure of ill people and directs this information to them in a dream which can then be related to their physicians.

3. Proceedings of the Parapsychological Institute of the State University of Utrecht, No. 3, January 1965, pp. 4, 5.

Augustus Caesar had a clairvoyant dream in which three Roman legions were destroyed in Germany by barbarians. One week later, dispatches confirmed to the Emperor that the destruction of the three legions had indeed taken place on the very evening of his dream.

In 1774, the Abbé Alfonso di Liguori had a clairvoyant dream in which he "attended" the bedside of Pope Clement XIV, who was dying in Rome —a week's travel from di Liguori's residence in Northern Italy. His description of the deathbed scene was accurate in every detail, including the number and the ages of the people "attending" the Pope.

Is a clairvoyant the same as a "medium," a "psychic," or a "sensitive?" What is meant by clairaudience? "Clairvoyant, medium, psychic, sensitive are interchangeable terms, but there are subtle differences," explains Ruby Yeatman. "For instance, a clairvoyant, although seeing things or scenes independently of the normal vision, may not be receiving information from a departed person, whilst a medium, in the fully used sense of the word, is or may be a channel for communication from the departed and at the same time may be possessed of clairvoyant and precognitive powers. A psychic and/or sensitive may be clairvoyant or precognitive or receive impressions regarding a person's health or character but is not in touch with the Unseen World. Clairaudience is the faculty of hearing sounds inaudible to the normal ear."

Is it true that we are all born with some degree of psychic power? Sharing the belief of many, Ruby Yeatman answers: "Generally one is born with psychic gifts of one kind or another, although some may be acquired. Usually those born with the gift are the most successful."

A well-known contemporary psychic is Uri Geller. The following example of his extraordinary clairvoyant abilities is from David Hammond's book *The Search for Psychic Power*: "Uri was asked to guess the face of a die [one of a pair of dice] shaken in a closed steel box. The box was vigorously shaken by one of the experimenters and placed on a table. The position of the die was *not* known to the researchers. Uri provided the correct answer eight times. The probability that this could have occurred by chance was about *one in a million*. The experiment was performed ten times, but Uri declined to respond two times, saying his perception was not clear." It might be easier to accept the fact that Uri Geller has clairvoyant ability than it is to accept that he could have guessed by a "one-in-a-million" chance.

When is clairvoyance likely to happen? Anyone may have a clairvoyant vision at any time—even if they have never experienced it before. My husband had a clairvoyant experience in 1956, while attending college in New Jersey. He recalls what happened that summer day:

"It was my normal habit, after class, to meet with friends for a game of bridge. On this particular July day, I begged off and did something which I had never done before. To this day, I dislike afternoon naps, but on that day I elected to go back to my room to take one. While I was lying on the couch, I suddenly saw one ship colliding with another. I clearly saw the name of the steamship *Andrea Doria*, while the other ship was flying under a Swedish flag. The vision continued and I saw the *Andrea Doria* sinking, people taking to lifeboats and others drowning. About a half an hour later, a friend knocked at my door to tell me he was going to meet a girlfriend who was arriving in New York aboard the *Andrea Doria*. I had not known that she was in Europe or that he was going to meet her; in fact, I did not know the girl at all. As soon as he mentioned the name *Andrea Doria*, I told him that the ship was sinking. My friend hurriedly left for New York, where he learned that the ship on which his girlfriend was to arrive was sinking off Nantucket, Rhode Island, having been hit by the Swedish liner *The Stockholm*."

And from *On ESP* by Robert H. Curtis comes this account:

"I lived fourteen miles from Memphis, Tennessee. One day I went to town to see a movie. I had an uneasy feeling as I entered the movie. All of a sudden I saw a fire on the screen and recognized it to be my house. The sight grew more vivid until I could endure it no longer. I left the movie with an overpowering pull that drove me homeward. Within a mile of home, I saw the fields all black and smoking. A boy hunting rabbits had thrown a lighted match in the field and started a fire. It took the fire department and 50 volunteers to save my home."

THAT is clairvoyance.

In closing this chapter, I would like to present a philosophical concept held by many for a number of years. Along with them, I strongly believe that man's unconscious perceives far more than his consciousness will admit. I think man is potentially capable of going back through time "mentally" and remembering all the experiences that have ever happened to him and his progeny. I also feel that man can perceive everything that is happening not only on earth but in the universe. Further, I am sure man is capable of "reading" the future. In other words, if man can "see" by going back in time mentally, he is also capable of mentally going forward into the future.

When the barriers that society has placed on man's mental capabilities are dropped, some of these incredible perceptions slip through. We label them forms of ESP: retrocognition, telepathy, clairvoyance, premonition, or precognition. It is hoped that one day all of man's thought, whether past, present, or future, can be accepted as the natural inheritance from our Creator.

Psychometry

One of the best practitioners of the ESP talent of psychometry was Eileen J. Garrett. In her book *Many Voices* she recalls her first experience with this gift:
"He had me hold a folded letter in my hand and then asked me to tell him what I knew about it. Since I felt certain that I could know nothing about it anyway, I thought it would be 'safe' to tell him the first story which came to my mind as I held the letter. In what sounded to me like a vivid burst of imagination, I spoke of this man's father, of the father's desire to show that he had kept contact with his children, mentioning them by name. It turned out the letter had actually been written by his father, who had recently died and to whom he was extremely devoted."[1]

Perhaps one of the most dramatic examples of psychometry is described by D. Scott Rogo in *Parapsychology; A Century of Inquiry*:
"Senora Zierold was given a piece of string that originally had been attached to some dog tags worn by a German soldier: 'It is intensely cold and the day is foggy. . . . I am on a battlefield, it smells of gun powder. In front of me a tall man standing, with a gray overcoat on, which reaches to his feet. Behind him I see three other men standing likewise. They talk German, or better said, they shout. In front of them and lying on the snow, behind an earthwork, I see lines of soldiers keeping up a continuous rifle fire. Some five meters back of the fire line there are two groups of men plainly to be seen, one consisting of about 5 or 6 men, and another about 12 to 15 men. Quite of a sudden I see coming through the air and moving with great rapidity a big red ball of fire . . . which drops just in the middle of the 15 men tearing them to pieces.' "[2]

Senora Zierold's description of the war scene emanated from the string she held. It belonged to a German soldier who had written home about his "first great impression . . . received of the war"—during the Battle of

1. Garrett, *Many Voices*, pp. 50, 51.
2. Rogo, *Parapsychology*, p. 156.

Flanders, in December 1914. Senora Zierold held the string in her hand and gave the above impression of the battle in the summer of 1924!

What is psychometry? Psychometry has been defined as "a means of picking up information about a person or events—past, present, and future —from an inanimate object"[3] and as "a psychic power possessed by certain individuals which enables them to divine the history of, or events connected with, a material object with which they come in close contact."[4]

The word *psychometry* is taken from the Greek, and literally translates as "the measure of the soul." Although today the term is used to represent object reading, many exponents of the talent state that *inanimate objects do have souls.* Further, they claim *these objects give off electrical impulses or emanations*—much the same way that animate objects (people, flowers and plants, fish and animals) do. According to this theory, when a sensitive or medium is touching an object, he or she is "measuring the soul" of that object and divining its history—past, present, and future.

When was the term "psychometry" first used to describe this psychic ability? The term *psychometry* was used initially by Dr. James Rhodes Buchanan in 1849. He was probably the first person to demonstrate that an inanimate object could be a carrier of ESP knowledge. He experimented with nonprofessional subjects and found that some of them could accurately identify different medicines concealed in locked boxes simply by rubbing the boxes. The successful subjects were later given handwritten letters and again they were accurate in giving complete descriptions of the writers. When Dr. Buchanan published his finding in a medical journal, he coined the word *"psychometry"* to explain this then astonishing ability.

What happens during a psychometric reading of an object? The experience of the reader is perhaps best decribed by Eileen Garrett:

"A coin is concealed in an envelope and held in the hand as a clew. As I hold the coin lightly, the actual presence of the person who has given it to me fades out, and the object takes on increasing importance. A tingling sensation announces that inner expectancy has begun and the coin begins to reveal its story. I may have a glimpse of a stately columned building standing on a height. People are passing in and out of it and moving about in its vicinity—Greeks of an ancient time. This is a temple of Aesculapius. I see his statue here—he wears a long robe, his breast is bare, he holds the symbolic staff with its twining serpent. The picture changes and I am in a dark cave from which I look out on a wide blue sea empty and beautiful under a pale sky. I *feel* that there are coins scattered on the floor of the cave, but it is too dark to see them. Then I see a glass case in which various coins are exhibited. All of these things—the temple and its statue, the cave, the glass case—are seen clairvoyantly; they require interpretation. So, summing up my experience, I consider the sequence in reverse order, as to time, and I say that the coin is a museum piece, an ancient Greek minting (I cannot decipher its date), that it was found in a cave in

3. Hammond, *The Search For Psychic Power*, p. 10.
4. Litkei, *ESP*, p. 19.

Greece, and that one of its owners—probably the last one—was a wealthy Greek, possibly a physician, but in any case a devotee of the god Aesculapius."[5]

The envelope did indeed contain a coin of ancient Greek origin.

How does psychometry work? In correspondence with Ruby Yeatman, she offered the following explanation:

"It is believed that every material object or article carries with it an influence, or aura, permanently, which can be sensed, or 'read,' by the sensitive who is possessed of this peculiar psychic faculty. Such a sensitive, given, for instance, a stone or tablet or some other article belonging to ages past, can give a description of the circumstances in which that article originally existed and the happenings which occurred at the time, and can describe people connected with it at different periods of its existence. Campbell Holms describes Psychometry as 'the peculiar clairvoyant faculty which enables certain mediums, while in the normal state, to perceive incidents' connected with any particular object. Dr. Eugene Osty in his book *The Faculties of Man* gives many instances of striking psychometric work, by sensitives with whom he had been in touch in experimental work. The thoughts, words, actions, and general circumstances connected with an article may be described by the sensitive holding the object."

Judith Richardson Haimes, the well-known aura-reading psychic, describes it this way:

"When you do psychometry, you pick up an article. You feel this article. Clairvoyantly, you will see something attached to this aura, and you may clairaudiently hear something. But only with an article which has had a very strong emotional movement around it. You may wear the same ring for three weeks and I pick it up, and pick up absolutely nothing, because nothing unusual has happened. You may pick up my ring and while you are holding it, there is an earthquake. And somebody else picks up that ring to psychometrize it, and they pick up the earthquake—they don't pick up you."

Are there certain conclusions that can be drawn about all psychometric readings? According to Dr. Raynor C. Johnson, there are four generalizations that can be made about psychometry:

"1. Each individual who has touched the article may be cognised without any confusion of persons and attributes.

"2. Once the rapport has been established the object has no further part to play and could be destroyed.

"3. The life of the subject can be cognised as it is in the present, irrespective of the time interval since the object was touched by that person.

"4. Objects placed in contact do not apparently communicate their peculiar psychic qualities to each other."[6]

5. Garrett, *Adventures in the Supernormal,* p. 125.
6. Johnson, *Psychical Research,* p. 66.

Many psychics agree with Dr. Johnson's thesis that once the object has been touched and has given off its emanations it no longer plays a part in the medium's or sensitive's readings. However, Mrs. Garrett claimed that the longer she kept the object in her hands, the more information she obtained from it. She strongly felt the object could tell the history of everything it had gone through; the characteristics of all its owners, and further, the future of the object itself and of those who would come into possession of it.

Personally, I feel that there is something in time and space or the great beyond that amounts to a reproductive system of everything that has ever happened in the universe. The sensitive who practices psychometry is merely the human instrument who tunes into this universal system and produces fragments of the past. Each object, whether animate or inanimate, carries its history within its "soul." And it would appear every soul is in tune with the pulsating universe that represents creation.

To what use can psychometry be put? Imagine, if a medium or sensitive can touch an object belonging to an individual and achieve a strong rapport with that person, all that can follow! Here is a potential method of both physical and mental diagnosis of illnesses—and the prospective patient need not be present. The person can be helped without his even knowing that a diagnosis has taken place. Although 100 percent accuracy may be extremely rare in psychometry, how many doctors can give 100 percent reliable analyses in the office, even with the patient present?

An area in which psychometry has already been successful is crime detection. Many sensitives are helping police departments in the United States and abroad to solve all types of crimes, from robbery to murder. Sensitives are given simple pieces of evidence and often are able to reconstruct the entire series of events around the crime, leading the police to the criminal. Other areas in which psychometry can be used are now being explored, but for those of health and criminal investigation psychometry is already a useful tool.

Psychometry also has been used very successfully to find missing persons, and to unearth lost wills or testaments.

Is there a possibility of error in psychometry? In an interview with the distinguished Professor W. H. C. Tenhaeff, Director of the Parapsychological Institute of the State University of Utrecht, Holland, he told of what some consider "errors" on the part of the sensitive, but which can be explained in this manner:

"It may occur that a paragnost [psychometrist] supplies particulars, which, though correct from the parapsychological point of view, nevertheless prove to be of no value from the point of view of the police.

"Something of this kind occurs repeatedly when use is made of police dogs. I know of various cases in the course of which the dog went to a place where a missing person had stayed for some time (and not to the place where the missing person—or his body—actually was). From the point of view of animal psychology such 'errors' are entirely in order. One must not consider a dog at fault if he indicates such a place which may be irrelevant from the point of view of the police.

"Now it is a remarkable fact that when a sensitive (as has repeatedly happened) 'sees' a place where the missing person stayed shortly before he met with an accident, and obtains no further impression, this will cause a number of people to speak with contempt about the performance of this paragnost.

"Such people, who only have an eye for practical results, cannot see that the mere fact that the paragnost was able to get an impression of the place where the missing person stayed for a time must be regarded as a remarkable paranormal performance."[7]

Are there professional "psychic detectives," and how do they operate? There are a few. One well known here and abroad is Peter Hurkos. His career began in Holland when he helped the local police find a missing girl simply by touching a handkerchief she had owned and telling the Dutch police where they could locate her body. When he ultimately helped track down the girl's murderer, his reputation was established.

His next sensational case was that of finding the Coronation Stone of England (better known as Stone of Scone), which had been removed from Westminster Abbey by Scottish Nationalists. British authorities, who had read about Hurkos' work in the Netherlands, contacted him to help solve the crime. Four weeks after he arrived in London, he told Scotland Yard where the Coronation Stone could be found. It was recovered in the place Hurkos described.

When asked to describe his ability of psychometry, Hurkos explained: "It's like watching a movie. I have to forget my private life, my family life. I have to blank everything out. Then I get this feeling and somehow make mental pictures. If I'm emotionally upset, though, I'm not worth a dime. Or when people tell me things about themselves, I become confused. The best way is not to tell me anything; just give me the object, that's when I get my best results."[8]

In the United States, Peter Hurkos is best known for his consultations with the Massachusetts police, leading to the identification, capture, and conviction of the so-called Boston Strangler. Further, he worked with the Miami Detective Department in locating "Murph the Surf" and the Star of India sapphire, which he allegedly had stolen from the American Museum of Natural History in New York City. Hurkos also helped find a missing doctor in Arizona and a missing child in Buffalo, New York.

All of these findings were accomplished through psychometry.

Aura-reading psychic Judith Richardson Haimes donates twenty to forty hours per week to working with the police and the FBI. She describes how she uses her talents in this area; "The police hand me an object and I will be able to pick up the violence, the strong emotions, and sometimes I

7. Proceedings of the Parapsychological Institute of the State University of Utrecht, No. 1, December 1960, p. 22.
8. Hammond, *The Search for Psychic Power*, p. 79.

am able to get a word clairaudiently, but let them hand me a photograph, and then I immediately see the aura and I know this color means this and this, and the puzzles of the picture fit together."

During an interview with Alex Tanous, well-known psychic and author of *Beyond Coincidence*, he stated that when practicing psychometry he "taps into the universe." Alex cited an instance in which his psychometry ability helped solve a murder:

"A girl had been found in New Jersey in the water, tied with chains. The police didn't know who had killed her. The crime was committed in 1969. This past summer [1976], the police obtained permission from New Jersey authorities to okay my being brought in to work on the case. The police brought to me, at the American Society for Psychical Research, the things the girl was dressed with when they found her in the water. I touched the objects and relived the whole crime. I then drew a sketch of the man who had committed the crime. The girl's energy was on the chains and it translated itself through me. I was able to relive the entire event and solve it for them. The man was already in jail for another crime. When they matched my sketch with the picture of the man they had, it was an exact duplicate."

I asked Alex how he felt when he experienced reliving a terrible crime such as murder. He replied that the feeling he undergoes is similar to the way one would feel while viewing a movie. His role is that of an observer. I inquired if Alex was equally able to discern crimes that had not yet occurred, and he stated he works with police in this connection as well.

A great number of psychics have turned their talents to help in parapsychological criminology. In Denver, a group of gifted psychics, covering the gamut of the field from clairaudience to psychometry, have formed the Rocky Mountain West's pioneer psychic investigatory team under the auspices of Lou Wright, a well-known psychic. Their aim is to help police on what appear to be dead-end cases.

It would be interesting to see what might happen if it were known to the public that a battery of psychometrists were available to the police to solve crimes. Possibly this could act as a strong deterrent to crime.

Can a person be psychometric without possessing any other psychic abilities? As has been indicated earlier, it is doubtful that any of the ESP talents exist in isolation. Dr. Alex Tanous believes that most, if not all, of his psychometric experiences are out-of-body projections. He uses the object on the order of a guidepost, similar to a road sign. It would appear that psychometry also makes use of many of the psychic forces that constitute the area of ESP—telepathy, clairvoyance, and possibly retrocognition. In any event, it has been shown that psychic abilities can be a source of help in many areas vital to the well-being of mankind.

CHAPTER
10

Psychokinesis

Although I personally have never experienced an example of psychokinesis, I have included a discussion of this ESP talent because I feel
psychokinesis (PK) is too important and too controversial to be over-
looked. Let's begin with some examples garnered from my research to
illustrate what PK is.

"One Illinois woman wrote . . . that at the exact time of her mother's
death an antique clock suddenly stopped. The clock stopped at the same
time the next day. Three years later it stopped again, signifying the birth of
a grandchild, and a fourth time when another child was married. In this
case it does seem that the woman herself was able to use her psychokinetic
ability to carry out a symbolic act to bring an ESP impression to consciousness."[1]

"My father and I are living in Isere. One of our friends was seriously ill,
and each day we expected to see him die. One evening, after having paid
him a visit, we had gone to bed fairly tired (for he lived three or four
kilometres from our home). Scarcely were we in bed when a violent blow
was struck on the head of the bed, and the curtains were set in motion by
an inexplicable puff of air. My father leaped out of bed, saying, 'He is
dead!' He looked at the time, and dressed himself hastily, that he might go
back to his friend. The latter had died at the moment when we heard the
blow and felt the puff of air."[2]

*How does psychokinesis work on a conscious level? On an unconscious
level?* On the conscious level: A person comes into a room, looks at a
glass on a table some ten feet away from him, and wants the glass to rise.
He is thinking about it consciously and the glass rises.

On the unconscious level: A person comes into a room and because of

1. Rogo, *Parapsychology*, p. 176.
2. Ibid., p. 175.

his great psychokinetic power, can cause the same glass to rise and fly through the air without thinking about it.

". . . I have seen a bunch of lilacs thrown onto a central table with never a murmur of telltale bells, never a flicker of the sensitive electric light that would have flashed if Stella [the medium] or any one of us had moved in our chairs. . . . I have seen a one-hundred-and-twelve-pound table lifted to the ceiling of the room, there to hang suspended while the best efforts of the group could not bring it down—but when at last it fell, it was ripped apart in the falling," recalls the psychic Eileen Garrett.[3]

How would you define psychokinesis? Psychokinesis, also known as tele-kinesis, can best be described as a person's ability to change or influence a physical object or happening by the use of his or her mind. In other words, someone *thinks* of trying to stop a clock and the clock stops. Someone *thinks* of trying to influence the throw of dice and the dice are influenced.

Does psychokinesis differ substantially from the ESP talents previously mentioned: telepathy, precognition, clairvoyance, and psychometry? In psychokinesis, a person influences a physical object or event by concentrat-ing on it. This thought can be either on the conscious or the unconscious level. He or she *causes* or *influences* an event to occur. The subject changes the external world by his mental ability. In the other forms of ESP, the subject himself is either reacting to or being influenced by the external world. It comes down to a matter of control. In psychokinesis, *you are in control.* In telepathy, precognition, clairvoyance, etc., *you are being con-trolled.*

What deductions can we make about PK regardless of the level on which it is operating? (1) It many times takes place during a period of emotional crisis. (2) It may be caused by either the subject or the percipi-ent. (3) It often expresses itself in a "symbolic" rather than a "real" form. (4) It represents the strongest form of "mind over matter" known to man.

What is the controversy surrounding psychokinesis? While most scien-tists might agree with parapsychologists on the existence of telepathy, precognition, and clairvoyance, the two groups part company on the talent of psychokinesis. Scientists can accept the theories of the emotional crisis and dual causality (the notion that the end is affected by two different causes) and probably the concept of "symbolistic-formulae (something that can be expressed in no other form than by symbol)." However, when it comes to acknowledging the possibility of "mind over matter," a number of scientists consider this too "far out" to discuss, much less attempt to evaluate.

What prompted this skepticism? Some of this skepticism remains as a legacy from the period 1880–1925, when there was strong belief in spir-

3. Garrett, *Adventures in the Supernormal*, p. 157.

itualism. It was a time during which the physical medium ruled surpreme —and, to the embarrassment of the devoted, many times was discovered to be a fraud. It was also a time of some serious investigation into the psychic world.

The eminent British physicist Dr. William Crookes performed a number of psychokinetic experiments from 1880 to 1900, which were hailed by many of his colleagues. Dr. Raynor C. Johnson, in his book *Psychical Research*, shares these observations from Crookes' journals:

"Crookes records numerous examples of heavy objects being moved at some distance from the medium (D. D. Home). He refers to five occasions on which he had seen a heavy dining-room table rise between a few inches and 1½ feet from the floor under special circumstances which rendered trickery impossible. Crookes mentions that there were at least a hundred recorded instances of the levitation of D. D. Home, and that he witnessed three of them. 'On three separate occasions I have seen him raised completely from the floor of the room; once sitting in an easy-chair, once kneeling on his chair, and once standing up. On each occasion I had full opportunity of watching the occurrence as it was taking place.' "[4]

"Crookes also states that in his own house where trickery or any sort of fraudulent preparation were quite out of the question, he had witnessed an accordion play in his own hand while he held it with the keys downward, and he had seen and heard the same accordion float about the room playing all the time. He claims to have seen a water-bottle and tumbler rise from the table, a coral necklace rise on end, and a fan move about and fan the company."

There are many more examples of some rather extraordinary events that were purported to have occurred: trumpets blowing and floating through the air; tables levitating and moving rapidly from one room to another; bowls of fish appearing out of thin air; mediums in trance levitating themselves several feet above the floor.

These curious and inexplicable manifestations of the powers of PK led a good number of scientists to turn away from psychokinesis for many years. It has only been within the past decade that the scientific community has given it any serious consideration—and this "serious" consideration is still in its infancy.

I do not mean to deny the validity of psychokinesis, for scientists have been wrong about many things throughout history. I am merely setting forth the controversial nature of this ESP talent. It would appear the mind has shown a great ability to gather facts and translate this information into action. *If this information can activate extramental abilities, may it not also activate extramuscular abilities which can combine with the mental to perform "incredible" feats of movement through space now unknown to man? Maybe we should include "motor" activity in ESP as well as "sensory" activity.*

Let me quote the great psychic Eileen J. Garrett, a skeptic if ever there was one:

4. Johnson, *Psychical Research*, pp. 79–80.

"Many learned men have testified to the genuineness of raps, movement of objects without visible means, and ectoplasmic substances, all of which come under the heading of physical phenomena. Notwithstanding, there are many who do not believe such things occur, but I am convinced partly by the large amount of evidence which has been made available from many sources, and partly because I have exposed to them myself."[5]

Who are the people currently responsible for psychokinesis being taken more seriously? One of the most remarkable practitioners of this talent living today is Uri Geller. In 1973, David Hammond had several lengthy interviews with the young Israeli psychic, a portion of which follows:

"I first met Uri on 27 March 1973 when he was interviewed for an article in *Psychic*. I was curious about his psychokinetic abilities that were said to bend metals and make objects dematerialize and rematerialize. I knew that the 26-year-old Israeli had performed a number of tests at Stanford Research Institute for physicists Harold E. Puthoff and Russell Targ under rigorously controlled conditions. . . . Shortly after the interview Ann Porter, *Psychic*'s assistant to the publisher, offered Uri a flower which he held in his hand for a few seconds. It became withered and dry. Amidst some nervous allusions to a similar fate perpetrated on a fig tree by one of Uri's progenitors (as recorded in the Gospels of Matthew and Mark), Ann then held a nail clipper in her hand while he made a motion with his hands over hers. When she opened her hand, she found the small blade broken off at the joint. That evening at dinner, Uri sat opposite me. As he was reaching for his water glass, his spoon of heavy silverware snapped in two."[6]

And to show yet another facet of Uri Geller's talent in this area, Hammond related an incident involving astronaut Ed Mitchell:

"Geller asked for someone's watch and Ed Mitchell gave him his. It was a rather complex watch that astronauts use. He asked Ed to hold the watch between his hands, and Uri then waved his hands on top of Ed's for a few seconds and then told Ed to open his hands. The hands of the watch had gone ahead about an hour or an hour and a half."[7]

Alex Tanous, the well-known psychic who recently has been participating in scientific studies at the American Society for Psychical Research with Dr. Karlis Osis, keeps his psychokinetic energies under tight control. "When I was asked to move a pen on a TV show, I refused," Tanous asserted. "I explained that if I could move the pen at will, then I can destroy at will and I am not ready for the responsibility of this. In other words, I am a builder. I believe in creativity. It seemed on TV, every time you were asked to do something in psychokinesis you had to bend a key or something similar, and that is not my bag. I told the master of ceremonies on the TV program that I would show him something close to PK—or telekinesis. I asked him to get a deck of cards, which he did. I asked him to open it. I told him that if I could command things to move, similarly I

5. Garrett, *Adventures in the Supernatural*, p. 157.
6. Hammond, *The Search for Psychic Power*, p. 26.
7. Ibid., p. 28.

could command something from him. I asked him to shuffle the cards and take away the jokers. While still on camera, I told him I would take a pad and write two cards down, and then command his mind to cut me one of those two cards. When he cut the cards, there was a jack. We then looked at what I had written on the pad. There was a jack and an ace. The TV host then asked me, 'Can you now make me cut the ace?' I said, 'Yes.' He then cut the cards and the ace appeared. That is a kind of PK. There is no destruction here, so I can take that responsibility." This is the type of work Alex Tanous does with retarded children, using the energy constructively to allow the children to be creative. Alex believes in this respect that "we are on the horizon of a new birth of the mind, which is expressing itself in many ways."

To what beneficial uses can PK energy be put? As incredible as psychokinesis sounds, the principle can lead to all sorts of human development. After all, if mental energy can move objects—regardless of their weights—there is literally no limit to what man can accomplish. Can he not move stones weighing as much as a thousand tons to build skyscrapers, stadiums, and bridge spans over great rivers? Historians have always pondered upon the building of the Great Pyramids in Egypt, Stonehenge in England, and the Tower of Babel. Psychokinesis suggests one possible explanation.

This ESP talent is in its infancy, so it would seem. Or is it that it exists, again, with the aid of that "Universal Current," which is part of so many other ESP talents as well as psychic healing? The direction it will take is anyone's guess. With a stretch of the imagination, psychokinesis and the energy it provides could take the place of both solar and atomic energy.

One might pause here to reflect upon the old adage that "wishing will make it so" and recall the philosophy that anything the mind is capable of thinking can become a reality. It is hoped that the wishes made in all the wishing wells in countries throughout the world will be geared toward the betterment of mankind.

11

Synchronicity

You have read in earlier chapters how I initially met Eileen Garrett, the famous medium and psychic researcher, in the lobby of my apartment building and how I also said goodbye to her in the same lobby where we had first greeted each other. These incidents heralded an interesting experience of my own:

My husband had an eye problem for which our doctor had a laboratory test performed. Since the doctor's visiting hours were until a certain time and my husband could not be home until after that, we agreed I would pick up the test results. Sitting in the waiting room of the doctor's office, I picked up a magazine and turned to a page which had printed on it in large letters the words *"E. coli."*

Some moments later, the doctor's door opened, and several people exited, followed by the doctor. He paused a moment when he saw me, almost as if he expected me to say something. The people—a man, a woman, and a young teen-age girl and boy—went out into the lobby. The doctor turned to me and asked, "Why didn't you say hello to them?" "I don't know them," I replied. He answered, "They are Eileen Garrett's daughter, son-in-law, and grandchildren." And so, I went out into the lobby, and introductions were made. The daughter's name was Eileen Coly —E. Coly—and when I returned to the doctor's office, I picked up the magazine to show him the large letters *"E. coli"* and remarked on the coincidence of meeting an "E. Coly." He then said to me, "Wait until you hear your husband's laboratory report—they say it is *E. coli*." (*E. coli* is a bacterial infection of a persistent nature.)

The mathematical probability that I would meet not only Eileen Garrett in this lobby, but also her daughter, son-in-law, and grandchildren—in the same lobby—and then have three related "coincidences" concerning *E. coli*—is staggering.

Prior to a diagnosis of my cancer illness, one might say that telepathically I had communicated a need for a clue to my neck and health problems. Mrs. Garrett's appearance in the lobby and my knowing her name even before we met provided that clue (remember my garroting dream).

Similarly, perhaps a telepathic communication was waiting for some corroboration of what was wrong with my husband's eye. Hence, Eileen Coly provided the clue to the medical problem of *E. coli*.

However, also consider the coincidence of the clue providers being mother and daughter, and the fact that the results of the laboratory test were delivered at the time E. Coly visited the doctor. I believe these events could be called "meaningful coincidences," for which Dr. Carl Jung had coined the term "synchronicity." In any event, that lobby certainly has something going for it!

An intriguing example of synchronicity was related by Andrea Fodor Litkei, daughter of the renowned and highly respected parapsychologist and author Dr. Nandor Fodor, in her book *ESP: An Account of the Fabulous in Our Everyday Lives.*

"I had been having numerous telephone conversations with Dr. Andrija Puharich, author of the best seller *The Sacred Mushroom* and *Beyond Telepathy.* He was a close friend of my father but I had met him for the first time only about a week previously. We were discussing an intriguing psychic possibility regarding my father, Dr. Nandor Fodor, who died May 17, 1964. Also, during that week I had painted a symbolic presentation of the 'sacred mushroom,' but this had nothing to do with Dr. Puharich or our discussions. I was on the verge of inviting him to dinner but had not made up my mind regarding the exact date, and terminated one of our conversations on this note.

"I walked into the living room and glanced at five azalea plants that I have on my window ledge among eighteen other plants and, to my utter amazement, found mushrooms growing out of one of the azalea pots. (This pot is situated in the brightest sun on the window ledge on a very high floor.) Since Dr. Puharich is a 'mushroom expert' I rushed to call him back and invited him to dinner on the spot to determine whether they really are mushrooms, and whether it is possible for this to happen.

"According to Dr. Puharich, if one tried to grow mushrooms in a very damp, dark basement one might succeed but the outcome would still be in doubt. He threw up his hands, saying that he had no explanation and to wait and see what would happen."

In an interview with Andrea she elaborated on the above events:

"Since mushrooms supposedly leave spores, after having removed these I expected more to grow. Altogether they grew out three separate times in only this one pot during the ensuing three weeks that my telephone conversations continued with Dr. Puharich. The minute these conversations ceased, not another mushroom grew, and I am still pot-watching to see if they will come again."

What does Mrs. Litkei make of these coincidences?

"Here we have three isolated facts: my painting of the sacred mushroom which I had never attempted before, and probably won't again; my intense conversations with Dr. Puharich, emotion-toned because of my father; and the mushrooms. At that time, I had the azaleas for eight years or more. I could have done the painting six months earlier, and it was sheer accident that I met Dr. Puharich and had the resultant telephone conversations with him. Granted that it is, although against all odds, a physical possibility for these mushrooms to grow in such an unlikely place, the fact of the meaningful coincidence of the painting and Dr. Puharich puts this happening into the class of synchronicity."[1]

What is synchronicity and how does it differ from coincidence? The definition of "coincidence" as we know it is two simultaneous occurrences that fit together but are the result of pure chance. Carl Jung's concept of synchronicity was that synchronistic events were coincidences that were meaningful; that they were not caused by pure chance, and that most coincidences were part of the natural order of the universe.

Today, many parapsychologists define synchronicity as a series of two or more coincidences where more than the probability of chance occurs. Further, these coincidences should have a meaningful end. Although some synchonicities have been called "supernatural," there are a large number that apparently go beyond this category and still do not enter the arena of pure chance.

What is at work during synchronicity? From my own experiences, I have come to the conclusion that when a series of these "coincidences" occur, something other than chance is indeed added. Perhaps it is an unconscious desire to make contact with someone or something who can give physical and/or emotional comfort during a stressful time. In any event, this "something else" has many times led me to a solution of a lingering problem.

The story of Mrs. Robinson, which I related to you in the early portion of this book, is a good example of a problem solved by a meaningful coincidence happening at a crucial time. Prior to my operation for cancer, I had expected a Mrs. Robinson to arrive as a helper to put my house in order. The thought of having a helper named Robinson was a comforting one, since the name was special to me. When a Mrs. Graves arrived instead, the implications of the name Graves threw me into a tizzy of uncertainty and apprehension about the future. But because of the appearance of the nurse after my operation—whose name was Mrs. Robinson—a serious problem was resolved by a meaningful coincidence.

Further, by dreaming the word "garrote" and meeting Mrs. Garrett, the problem around my neck was certainly helped by meaningful coincidences.

As to Dr. Puharich and the mushrooms in Andrea Litkei's azalea pot, a sense of comfort may have been derived from the presence of an unusual manifestation of mushrooms, especially when looking for some sign of communication from her late father.

Is the end result—the "meaningful end"—always necessary to synchronicity? "In our own lives we come across so many instances that we dismiss with a shrug and label coincidence," wrote Andrea Fodor Litkei. "In other words, we are saying that if such and such were calculated according to the probabilities of chance then this event would be likely to happen according to these calculations. Especially if they are of no importance, or if there has been no positive outcome of the two events, then we

1. Litkei, *ESP*, pp. 22–23.

say, so what! But the mechanism of these synchronicities, meaningful coincidences without acausal effects, does not depend on the outcome. The outcome is important only to us—but if there is none, it does not detract from the phenomenon itself."[2]

To illustrate that the outcome of a "meaningful coincidence" is important only to the one experiencing it, Andrea cites this story:

"Professor Grondahl, a friend of my father who taught Norwegian literature at London University, told him of an illuminating incident: 'One day I had just succeeded in catching an underground train [subway]. I was halfway in the car when the door shut and pinned me. I squeezed through, sat down, wiped my forehead and opened a grammar. The first sentence on which my eye fell read: AND THE MISERABLE CREATURE WAS CRUSHED FLAT BY THE DOOR.

" 'This sentence is a highly unusual one in a grammar. The fact that it applied to me was very odd. But I don't think the grammar was psychic.' "[3]

How and why do synchronicities occur? In a recent interview, Andrea explained her view:

"I have had so-called synchronicities. Actually, synchronicity is merely a label given by Jung to a coincidence that is meaningful. We have very many coincidences that go by completely unnoticed because they don't change your life. They may not be meaningful at the time, but the principle of the coincidence or the synchronicity working does not change the fact that it happened merely because you don't notice it or it isn't meaningful. We are inclined to attribute that nothing matters unless it's meaningful to us. It happens regardless.

"We probably attract the synchronistic situation and put ourselves in it. In other words, the synchronicity, or the coincidence, happens. And, because we may have strong unconscious needs to fulfill whatever is in ourselves, or even conscious needs, we manage to put ourselves in that position at that moment where the synchronicity is going to happen . . . whether you are there or not . . . where more or less we draw ourselves toward it the same way as we draw things toward ourselves. And that is why I think it is almost impossible to calculate the question of chance happenings . . . because it will happen and you may not be there, and you will never know about it. In other words, only synchronistic happenings that we know about are ones that we are in and aware of."

What is the importance of synchronicity? I believe we should go back to Dr. Carl Jung for an appreciation of this. Jung, an eminent psychoanalyst, refused to accept his patient's experiences as mere "normal casuality." He expected his patients to respond to his treatment in a "meaningful manner." An example of this and his theory of synchronicity can best be described in the story of a female patient with a strong power complex, whom Jung considered a devouring personality. In one of her sessions with him, she repeated a dream that she had had several times. She saw three

2. Ibid., pp. 111–12.
3. Ibid., pp. 105–6.

tigers seated on straw threateningly in front of her. After the session, Jung told his patient to go for a long walk to calm down. She left the clinic with a friend and strolled along Lake Zurich, Switzerland. They noticed a crowd gathering in front of a barn. She and her friend walked over to the barn and were amazed to find three tigers in the building. Jung claimed that the woman's personality, as analyzed in his sessions with her, led to the dream . . . and then to the reality of the tigers . . . and then to the synchronicity.

You may question whether or not this was pure coincidence, but Jung states that no one could persuade this patient with her power complex that she was living in a purely naturalistic universe. She later told the doctor that something certainly had been added. This "something" was synchronicity. Jung refused to accept the so-called pre-established harmony of all events. He asserted that synchronistic events were caused by this extra something—that synchronicity was the equivalent of *meaningfulness in life.*

Perhaps when you and I say to each other, "Let's synchronize our watches," similarly "meaningful coincidences" are synchronized. Possibly it is as simple as that.

Are synchronistic experiences always serious? The experiences that inspired Dr. Jung to the theory of synchronicity have been serious, meaningful events. Most synchronicities are, because they're usually tied to stressful times. However, it's not always the case, as this lighthearted illustration of my own will demonstrate.

On Wednesday, September 22, I had lunch with John F. Raffa, a Vice President of the Chase Manhattan Bank. Prior to eating, I told him I had brought a box of candy for him, certainly an unusual thing for a lady to bring to a man. He said he had some candy in his drawer, as it happened. I replied that some friends of mine had just brought this particular box of candy from the Hershey, Pennsylvania, company where they had visited. When I handed him the box of candy, he laughed, opened his desk drawer, and pulled out an open box of the identically packaged candy, milk chocolate with almonds, from the Hershey Co. in Pennsylvania. He said friends also brought the box to him. I told him that since his box of candy had been opened and was almost finished, this box was probably meant to be the replacement—and certainly an interesting conversation piece!

Two friends, one his and one mine, who didn't know each other had gone to visit the Hershey factory in Pennsylvania, and both had brought back identical packages of candy. Added to that, John Raffa and I were both the surprise recipients of the candy. Consequently, I believe these coincidences can be classified as synchronicities.

Except for the numbers which appear on my bathroom scale, one might wish for more synchronicities with a "sweet tooth."

For the skeptics who have joined us in reading this book, it might be interesting to calculate the mathematical possibilities implied by the following case:

"The London newspaper reported on April 1st, 1930, that during the evening of the previous day two men, both named Butler, both butchers, were found (one in Nottinghamshire, one near London) shot by the side of their cars. One was named Frederick Henry Butler, and the other David Henry Butler. They were entire strangers, unrelated, and both shot themselves with pistols by the side of their cars.

"In a case like this there is no chance of expectation on which a calculation could be based. The expectation is infinitesimal. Were it to occur once in a billion of suicides with two strangers of the same occupation, of the same name under the same circumstances, even then there is nothing to tell the date at which the occurrence is likely to take place. It may as well happen today as a thousand years hence."[4]

This is synchronicity.

4. Ibid., pp. 107-8.

PART III

INTRODUCTION

The Trail Leads to the Spiritual

My interest in the "spiritual" began after a very unusual experience that occurred while I was in the midst of typing the final copy of my husband's master's thesis. In fact, the circumstances that surrounded the last few days before my husband took his oral examination and submitted his written thesis were intriguing.

For some weeks, I had been typing the material. When completed, it was to be given to the chairman of the committee, who would give my husband his orals. We learned in the eleventh hour that the chairman, Professor Edward McNall Burns, had been awarded a Fulbright Scholarship and was scheduled to leave for Germany on Labor Day, so the timing for my husband's examination had to be moved up two weeks. This left us with only two days for me to complete the typing, and for my husband to complete the studying.

That August was exceedingly hot, and the last night before the examination was particularly so. There was not a breath of wind. We had no air conditioner at the time. I threw open the windows and disrobed to only my slip. I continued typing and my husband continued studying. The hours rushed by. Finally, I suggested that my husband get some sleep, since it was approaching midnight, and he had to be fresh for the test. He said he had completed studying all but one part—the Constitution of the French Republic—but he understood he would not be queried on that section.

My husband then went into the bedroom and promptly fell asleep from exhaustion. A short time later, I became more uncomfortable with the heat. I moved my typing table nearer to the window. Still not a breath of air was stirring. I continued typing for about a half hour. Suddenly, a gust of wind swished into the room, causing the draperies to fly. The wind hit my face, and I had to quickly turn from its force. As I turned, for some unaccountable reason, I switched on a little radio next to my table. In an instant, there was music. I was astonished at my own action because I have never liked to listen to music when I work, as it distracts me.

A moment later, my husband appeared bleary-eyed and said the music woke him up. I apologized and as I reached to turn it off, he quickly caught my hand and said, "No, don't turn it off. That is Les Sylphides. It is the first record my mother ever bought me." (My husband's mother had died some years before, too soon to see fulfilled her dream of her son's obtaining his master's degree.) Since he was up, he decided to study the portion about the French Republic. The next day when he took his orals, he found one-third of the examination was on the French Republic, although he had been told by his professor that the tests would not deal with that area.

Had he not been awakened by the music and had he not then continued his studies into the area of the French Republic, my husband would not have passed his oral examination, and his mother's dream would never have been realized.

It would be nice to think that my husband's mother was able to help him in this fashion. But one must also wonder if there was some psychic energy within either my husband or myself which provoked that gust of wind. In any event, *whatever* caused the wind to suddenly appear, and the radio to be playing the first music recording given to my husband by his mother, it was a friendly force, or spirit, and an ultimate good was achieved.

The reader should be made aware that not a great deal should be anticipated by the sitter in a first meeting. I have described in the following chapters my interesting if not exciting visit with a sensitive at the College of Psychic Studies in England, in contrast to the very dramatic meeting my husband had with the same sensitive one year later. Regrettably, the United States does not at this time have a comparable establishment to serve as a training ground for sensitives and mediums. Such a program as the one sponsored by the College of Psychic Studies in London helps alleviate the possibility of fraud.

In this section we will explore the "spirit world"—its ghostly inhabitants and their earthbound liaisons, the sensitives or mediums—and how the two sides communicate. It is hoped that some of the information in these chapters will help you to understand a bit more about sittings, sensitives, and spirits.

Mediums and Sensitives

What is a medium? A medium is a person who functions as a go-between for you—the living, who want to get some information from a departed soul on the other side—and presumably the dead, who can provide that information.

In other words, the medium is a form of communication. The plural, "media," means all types of communication, such as television, radio, magazines, and newspapers.

What is the difference between a medium and a sensitive? Dr. Lawrence LeShan, the well-known author and psychic researcher, offers this definition from his book *The Medium, the Mystic and the Physicist*:

"A *sensitive* is a person who demonstrates precognition, telepathy and/or clairvoyance with unusual frequency. A *medium* is a sensitive who explains her (most frequently in Western culture these are women) acquisition of paranormally gained information by saying that she gets it from 'spirits' or 'the souls of people who have already died.'"

British psychic Don Galloway stated that a medium is mainly "attuned solely to the spirit world, who concentrates on endeavouring always to receive survival evidence more than anything else." Whereas a sensitive "is one attuned to the spirit world, but over a broader horizon of spiritual—rather than simply psychic—awareness; one who can perceive what we might call an individual's spiritual pattern of life." Don also thought the sensitive would be delicately attuned to the atmosphere, people's auras, and so on, "and very often works through a cross-weave of psychic emanations from the various levels, not always working with a conscious line of communication with a specific spirit personality as the medium does."

Generally speaking, the sensitive has a highly developed faculty of ESP, and usually directs this ability as he or she so determines. By this we mean that the sensitive does not go into a trance to receive information. He remains conscious and in control of his faculties and is therefore able to provide information through his own abilities.

On the other hand, the medium almost always has to go into a trance to provide information of a paranormal nature. When the medium goes into the so-called "dead-trance" state, he or she is temporarily possessed or taken over by a discarnate being—better known as a "control." The discarnate being is generally accepted to be a departed soul that has returned to earth for the purpose of communication.

Another belief held is that the "control" may be an offshoot of the unconscious mind of the medium. Still another view held is that there are thoughts from souls who have departed which remain forever in a so-called Universal Mind and that all communications received or sent via mediums are derived from that source.

Are there different types of mediums? How do they operate? Professionals in the field of ESP usually divide mediumship into two types: the physical medium and the mental medium.

When the physical medium goes into trance, he or she brings about physical phenomena. These may include psychokinesis, such as the lifting of a table, chairs floating through the air, glasses falling over, all without any physical means of movement. The medium is also capable, it seems, of producing materializations, or the appearance of a discarnate spirit, which appears in ghostlike forms.

When the mental medium goes into trance, he or she provides ESP information by the use of speech or writing. The information is presumed to come from a discarnate being or control.

Paul Beard, president of the College of Psychic Studies in London, had this to say about the various types of mediums:

"Mediums can be divided into physical or mental mediums. Very few physical mediums exist today but they would be expected to provide examples of the direct voice of the communicator, or to produce materialisations which consist of an image or replica of a dead person but which must not be confused with the dead person himself or herself, any more than a photograph or a cassette tape is to be confused with the person photographed or making the recording. Mental mediumship, as the name applies, is largely a form of telepathic exchange between a dead communicator or a living person and the sensitive. It is not always easy to distinguish whether the source of the medium's material lies in a living or a dead person. . . .

"A third form of mediumship is, of course, mediumship by way of trance, which is really a form of mental communication. It is often supposed in trance that the soul or inner self of the medium is removed from her body with a communicator or teacher stepping into the body and taking her place. This is beginning to be recognised as a misrepresentation of the actual situation, which can much better be compared to an overshadowing by a communicator whereby they are able to influence the aura of the medium and pass thoughts to the inner self of the medium, which the medium then interprets more or less in her words. It can be seen that a very high degree of attunement is necessary for this method to be fully productive. When the medium under trance apparently lapses into unconsciousness, it would be more accurate to say that a skilled communicator has the power temporarily to deaden the outer everyday mind of the medium. The degree of unconsciousness or comparative dimming of the outer mind can vary very greatly. Mediums in the early stages of developing the trance very often hear all that is being said by the communicator but find themselves unable to influence it. At a somewhat later stage they hear the voice of the communicator rather like one hears a ripple or a stream of traffic without being able to identify the actual meaning of the sentences spoken. At a further stage still they may be completely unconscious. The depth of the control can vary very greatly within the same interview. However, some aspect of the medium's mind and personality is always present and colours the communication, however deep the trance may be."

What are some phenomena associated with mediums? D. Scott Rogo gives some examples of trance phenomena and explains how the various types of mediumship work:
"Note that even though these phenomena are often exaggerated, they do contain the roots of ESP and PK [psychokinesis]. Although the form of these paranormal manifestations was gilded . . . it is more than suggestive that a real element of psi [psychic phenomena] pervaded them: rappings; spirit writing (appearance of writing independent of any human being such as on sealed slates); trance speaking (this would later turn into trance mediumship, a state wherein the psychic often demonstrates psi abilities); clairvoyance; luminous phenomena (lights and so forth which later would be well observed as a peculiar form of physical phenomena); spiritual impersonation (where the medium takes on the characteristics of a dead individual); spirit music (usually plucking strings on instruments often levitated, a form of telekinesis); visible and tactile manifestations. . . .
"Other phenomena included were apparitions; visions and previsions; dreams (psychic ones, it is presumed); presentiments (precognitive experiences); spirit influence; involuntary utterances while the psychic was still partially conscious (a form of trance mediumship); and possession (also a type of mediumship)."[1]

Is it true that there are very few physical mediums practicing today? What could account for this? Ruby Yeatman, formerly of the College of Psychic Sciences in London, claims this to be the case, and offers the following explanations:
"It is true, at any rate here in the British Isles and I believe elsewhere, that physical mediumship is to-day very rare," she said. "I do not think any reason has been definitely put forward to explain this but it could be that people are not born today with the special make-up, or psychic power, necessary for such mediumship. Again, it could be that those in the Unseen World responsible for the phenomena of Spiritualism generally feel there is no longer any need for this form of activity; it may have been used

1. Rogo, *Parapsychology*, pp. 49–50.

in the same way as the big drum of the Salvation Army is used—to attract attention—and it certainly did that in those years when it was so active. It drew attention to the presence of something Other.

"It may be also that two world wars have so disturbed the psychic atmosphere that the production of such phenomena has been seriously upset or made almost impossible.

"One other form of physical phenomena, which is partly physical and partly mental, is direct and independent voice. This is the hearing of voices supernormally produced and amplified by the use of a trumpet or trumpets. Independent voice is the hearing of voices supernormally produced away from the medium and without the use of a trumpet.

"Psychic photography is another activity which should come under the heading of both mental and physical mediumship. It is the appearance on a negative of a face or form which was not physically apparent to the experimenters."

When a living person wants to communicate with a "spirit" in the "Beyond," does he have to do it through a medium? "If the living person is not himself psychic, or a medium, then, with rare exceptions, he cannot communicate direct with a departed person but must perforce have the services of a reliable medium," affirmed Ruby Yeatman. "A person here and there does occasionally have the precious experience of communion, as distinct from conscious communication through a medium, with one who has died, but this is rare. Many a lover knocks on the door of death and gets no answer."

When a person talks with someone from "Beyond," does the spirit speak in its own voice? Or does it talk in the voice of the medium or a control? Is it a common occurrence for spirits to speak to living people? Ruby Yeatman answers: "When a spirit, or the Control of a medium, speaks to a person here (the sitter at a séance) it is the larynx and voice of the medium which is used, except in those rare cases (very rare today) when the medium is what is known as a direct voice medium (a form of physical mediumship, distinct from mental trance mediumship). It is only 'a common occurrence' for spirits to speak to living people if such living people visit mediums regularly, or, if the living person is a natural medium."

Undoubtedly a psychic or sensitive receives an infinite number of impressions. How does the psychic determine which are important and which are trivial? "The answer by and large is by trial and error," says Ruby Yeatman. "It is a matter of experience to be able to distinguish between the impressions which may be arising from the knowledge and information gathered by the conscious mind, the upwelling of similar knowledge from the sub-conscious and genuine psychic impressions being received either through the inherent psychic faculty of the sensitive or by impression, or influence, from a departed person in the unseen world. Those sensitives who believe they are receiving, or being helped (or guided) by some person or persons in the next world would mentally ask for help from that person, would quieten as far as possible the conscious mind, and would quietly and confidently await the impact of an impression which they would instinctively be able to recognise as the true one coming from a source other than their own mind. The sensitive has to "feel" that such and such an impression or statement is the true one. The psychic who relies solely upon himself, that is upon his own inherent psychic faculty, which can be and often is quite distinct from any form of impression from the Unseen, is perhaps more liable to be puzzled by what he received than is the other, unless exceptionally gifted."

If someone was told by a medium that she would die in a particular city, what credence should be given such a prediction? According to Paul Beard, president of the College of Psychic Studies in London:

"True communicators of good stature would be highly unlikely to make a specific precognition as to somebody's death, and if such is given it would be wise to give no credence at all to such a prediction. Sometimes a communicator gives a general warning, perhaps that it might be wise for a sitter to think about putting his affairs in order, but this falls into quite a different category from a specific prediction. A few cases are on record of a specific precognition of death having proved accurate to the day, but these are very rare. A communicator subject to good moral influences will not normally be allowed to make such a prediction. It is quite clear that spiritual laws exist which govern what may or may not be told to a sitter, but it is of course difficult for us to discover exactly what these laws are. It is probable that we are not intended to know a great deal about such laws, it being considered wiser that we live our lives out in accordance with our own moral principles and spiritual intuitions, and without becoming over-dependent on help from discarnate sources, particularly of a practical kind."

What determines if a person has the potential to become a medium? "Theoretically speaking" explains Paul Beard, "it might be true to say that every person has the potential to become a medium, in much the same way as every person has the potential to become a player of the violin. In both cases the amount of talent may be so small as to be useless to other persons. What is required in the early stages is the sensitivity to record impressions which may reach the potential medium either from living or from dead persons. A mediumistic impression is a very delicate thing and the link between medium and communicator can very readily be shattered. The quality which distinguishes the good sensitive—and good sensitives are very rare—is the ability to hold on to the thread from a communicator for just as long as may be required, perhaps ten minutes, twenty minutes, thirty minutes. Poor sensitives, including many who work upon the platform in small churches in England, are only able to hold on to a thread for a minute or two and thus are seldom able to pass on communications in depth. It is also extremely hard for a sensitive, and requires a good deal of training, to report exactly what they hear, and no more, because it is extremely easy to misinterpret, or to add a slant to the sensitive's own, without noticing that this is being done. A good sensitive has to be a very disciplined person indeed at their work and the majority of those training fail to provide the necessary dedication to reach the required standard."

How do mediums develop their skills? What kind of training do mediums undergo? Perhaps the best way to answer this question is to look into the background of one of the most talented mediums of the twentieth century—Eileen J. Garrett. The quoted material is from her book *Many Voices.*

Mrs. Garrett believed that her mediumship was the result of both her birthplace (Ireland) and her training (England). She felt that the people of Ireland were not only psychically gifted, but highly clairvoyant. The social and religious customs of the Irish people, which included the Celtic belief in leprechauns and spirits which inhabited the mountains and glens, created an individuality that was both imaginative and superstitious. Eileen felt that her spiritual consciousness concerning life and afterlife stemmed from this background.

Eileen's interest in mediumship began in England with a visit to the London Spiritualist Alliance. There she met Mrs. Mercy Phillimore, who told her: "The gift of mediumship belongs to one's basic being. Once these patterns 'break through,' they can be likened to a flowing river, and they cannot be shut off without creating some form of mental anxiety. The lack of pattern or ordered form in such sensitivity is troublesome, but it can be subjected to discipline and control."

Eileen received her training at the College of Psychic Sciences throughout the 1920s, where she worked with Hewat McKenzie, founder of the college, and his wife, Barbara. Although Eileen was primarily a trance medium, while in a London hospital for a bout with pneumonia, she underwent a period of physical mediumship. The phenomenon was to continue for a period of three weeks. In the beginning, the nurses who were attending Eileen heard only raps on the furniture in her room. These raps soon gave way to long intervals of strong violence. The doors to the room would blow open with a loud noise—apparently a great force was being applied against them. The furniture in the room began to shake and tremble and eventually the nurses saw this same furniture levitate more than one foot above the ground. Finally, the trembling of the bed in which Mrs. Garrett was hospitalized became so persistent that the nurses refused to attend her. After her recovery, Eileen mentioned these occurrences to Mr. and Mrs. McKenzie. They told her that it was an outbreak of physical mediumship. They went on to say that such outbreaks were common among trance mediums who were undergoing great stress and crisis situations. Mr. McKenzie told Eileen that she had the potential for fine trance mediumship. He warned her against becoming a physical medium and cautioned her about possession by discarnate spirits.

G. R. S. Mead, secretary of the Theosophical Society in London, expressed similar misgivings to Eileen: "The river of the subconscious may have overflown its banks in this time of mental suffering to produce physical mediumship." Mead calmed Eileen, assuring her that in time the pattern would settle down. He felt that the unusual emotional time of illness and melancholy could have produced the physical happenings.

The McKenzies continued working to sharpen Eileen's gifts as a trance medium. They strongly believed that hypnosis was the preliminary step to trance withdrawal. Eileen, however, was both uncertain and frightened about her mediumistic ability. She has said in many of her books that she enjoyed this hypnotic training because it helped her to overcome her uncertainties and fears in this area. In an effort to help her understand her controls, McKenzie offered a hypnotic suggestion:

"It is your duty as a trance medium to give yourself to the care and wisdom of your controls, who in turn are being trained by me. In this state you are relaxed, in a world apart from men and their anxieties. Your mind will become tranquil and calm to truly reflect the impressions which the controls will bring forth."[2]

After years of training, Mrs. Garrett became one of the leading trance mediums in England. She would frequently pass into a trance state and allow her "controls" to take over. The college used her abilities to aid people who came with serious questions and emotional problems dealing with both health and departed dear ones. Although Eileen questioned mediumship in general and her own ability in particular, she developed two important criteria on mediumship. The first involves proving the validity of a spirit message.

"If such messages [from the dead] are outside the medium's range of knowledge and are characteristic of the personality who communicates, it can be considered fair proof of the continued memory of the one who has died. . . . The question of mediumship largely turns upon proof of identity —the proof given through the sensitive must be clear and coherent."[3]

The second attests to there being nothing extraordinary about mediumship:

"My investigations of the phenomena of mediumship convince me that these are not new or extraneous sensitivities but rather refinements of the physical senses all men possess. I cannot therefore accept the usual explanation of mediumship as an abnormal or supernormal development."

In later years, Eileen claimed that a tremendous change in public attitude toward mediumship had occurred. The attitude of the 1920s and 1930s was one of skepticism and scoffing; the 1960s, however, saw both mediums and sensitives appearing on television. Eileen explained why she felt the change in public attitude had taken place:

"Apparently it [mediumship] is becoming more and more in demand as anxiety spreads within the populace. The enormous impact of this widespread concern brings forth the need to depart from religious formula toward a horizon of 'being certain.' That once one is within the summerland of participation with the living dead, all is well!"

2. *Many Voices*, p. 55.
3. Ibid., p. 67.

CHAPTER

13

Controls

Who or what are controls? In trance mediumship a phenomenon known as a control, or guide, generally appears as soon as the medium goes into a trance. The controls usually claim to be the discarnate spirits of those who have passed on. They assert that they are there to pass messages from the spirit world to those in the living world by using the medium's mind. In other words, the control is acting as the "go-between," while the medium is in this sleeplike stage.

But the experts don't all agree on this. Consequently, there are several schools of thought about this question: One faction embraces an acceptance of the control's claim to be a discarnate being. This view regards the control's function as a protection against the indiscriminate invasion of the medium's brain by other spirits. A second view sees the control as the creation of the medium's mind. This theory holds that the control is actually a secondary personality of the medium, which comes out when he or she is in the hypnotic-like trance. A third hypothesis states that when the medium enters into a trance, he or she tunes into either a Universal Psychic Record or a so-called Collective Memory, which contains everything that man ever did or knew. It is from this psychic record, its supporters claim, that the medium draws information from the world beyond.

In recent correspondence with Ruby Yeatman, she offered her definitions of a control and an explanation of why they are important:

"The Control of an entranced medium is usually someone who has passed over many years ago (sometimes hundreds) or, on the other hand, comparatively recently. 'Dr. Lang' the Control of George Chapman, the healing medium, died, I believe, in 1937; Patience Worth, who communcated through the American sensitive, Mrs. Curran, died 400 years ago. The Control acts as intermediary between the medium and sitter and the departed person who wishes to send messages or give evidence of his identity to the sitter and is not able to do so himself, not having mastered the technicality of communication. Many mediums never have direct communications from the departed friend of the sitter; it is always given by the Control, who is the door-keeper, and allows only those to communicate who should rightly be there. But, with some highly gifted mediums in trance, the Control will stand aside and allow the sitter's own friend or relative to take control and speak direct to the sitter, but even so it is the medium's voice which is used, except on a very rare occasion.

"A Control is important to act, as indicated as the door keeper and to help those who wish to communicate. There are mediums, however (comparatively few), through whom communication is given direct from the departed relative or friend to the sitter via the medium—no Control."

How do controls come by their names? As you will have observed in the above, the controls have distinctive names—e.g., "Dr. Lang" and "Patience Worth." These names are established by the controls themselves. In *Many Voices* Eileen Garrett recalled meeting her Control for the first time:

"I must have gone to sleep easily enough; on my awakening, the teacher informed me that he had spoken to one 'Uvani,' an entity or 'control' personality of oriental origin, who foretold that I would become the vehicle for this type of work and that for a number of years I would serve in the capacity of a trance medium."

Arthur Ford, the famous American medium, told about the first encounter with his trance control named Fletcher in an interview for *Psychic* magazine in 1970:

"Toward the end of 1924, when I was in a meditation group in New York . . . I went into a trance. . . . Suddenly I began to talk with a French accent. The voice [control] said his name was Fletcher and told who he was."

A remarkable British medium for more than fifty years, Estelle Roberts, gave a moving account of her first meeting with her control, Red Cloud:

"I was still trying to adjust myself . . . when I saw and heard my guide for the first time. A voice said in stilted, too-precise English: 'I come to serve the world. You serve with me, and I serve with you.'

"I asked, 'Who are you?'

"The voice replied, 'I am Red Cloud.'

"As these words were spoken, I saw the top part of a man's figure surrounded by a halo of white light. His skin was olive-colored, his eyes were dark, and he wore a small black beard. In that moment I was aware as surely as if Red Cloud had told me that all that had gone before in my past life—the privation, the long hours of manual work and particularly, my spirit voices—had been part of a preconceived pattern. And now the pattern was complete. I knew with unwavering certainty that my true mission in life—whatever it may be—had just begun."[1]

What happens when a control appears? How does the person experiencing this feel? Douglas Johnson, the renowned British medium, tells what it was like when he first became aware he had a control: "Chang first controlled me when I was a boy of about 16. I was with some Spiritualist

1. Roberts, *Fifty Years a Medium*, p. 27–28.

friends sitting quietly in their home group when I thought I had fainted. When I came to, they told me that I had been talking for about an hour. I was terrified and wondered if it would come on at school, or in a bus! . . . He [Chang] says he was my brother in an earlier life in China."

Queried about proof of the existence of his control, Douglas stated: "I cannot prove his existence and, of course, many psychologists think I do unconscious self-hypnosis and that Chang is a higher aspect of my personality. I believe him to be a separate entity. When asked if he felt the average person could go into trance, Douglas Johnson compared it with the possibility of the average person singing in opera: 'Psychic ability is a gift like music or painting, either born with you or not.' "

Can controls provide information about the future? "One may turn to the experiments of C. Drayton Thomas with the gifted psychic Gladys Osborne Leonard," says D. Scott Rogo. "Mrs. Leonard would enter a trance state during which a control (an alleged discarnate) would take possession of her. In some of the experiments the controls would be asked to describe passages from the following day's newspapers. The experiments were timed in such a way that the type would not yet have been set up or determined. Any success would have to be true precognition. Many of the experiments were strikingly successful."[2]

How do controls communicate? By telepathy, it is believed. Paul Beard, in his book, *Survival of Death*, asserts:

"Discarnate communicators, if we choose to believe them, make use of telepathy because it surpasses the limits of verbal communication and they say they do so not only when attempting to communicate with us on earth, but as a natural mode of expression between themselves."

In the following excerpt from a *Psychic* magazine interview, Arthur Ford explained what it's like when Fletcher, his control, wants to communicate:

"When Fletcher comes through, my conscious mind is completely out. So I don't consciously color the information. But everything that comes through me must be colored to some extent by what I know or what I think."

Can a medium have more than one control? In some instances, yes. For example, when Eileen Garrett went to the British College of Psychic Science to be trained as a trance medium, she worked under the tutelage of Hewat McKenzie, who soon identified that Eileen had two controls: "Uvani" and "Abdul Latif."

How do mediums feel about their controls? Do they trust and believe in them? A number of mediums, including Eileen Garrett and Arthur Ford, had difficulty accepting the existence of their controls.

All her life Eileen Garrett was to express concern and self-doubt about the identity of her controls. At times, Eileen accepted them for the discarnate personalities they claimed to be. At other times, she strongly felt

2. Rogo, *Parapsychology*, p. 142.

that they were secondary and even tertiary personalities of her own unconscious. But in her continuing search into the Great Beyond, Eileen sometimes stated that these same controls could be part of the Universal Mind that had existed before time and which would exist beyond time. Of her uncertainty she has said: "My own lack of a true belief in the identity of the controls troubled me. I had never been certain of their reality or that the messages they conveyed from their 'universe' about those who had departed this life were truly evidence of life after death."[3]

Is there any evidence to support or prove the existence of these spirit guides and their contact with the "other side"? There are countless, if intangible, examples of "proof" of the identity of controls. For example:

Eileen Garrett accomplished her work as a psychic healer with the help of her control, Abdul Latif. This control claimed to be a physician at the Turkish court of Saladin in the twelfth century. Sir Arthur Conan Doyle, who was a psychic experimenter and spiritualist, and R. H. Saunders coauthored a book entitled *Health, Its Recovery and Maintenance*. The book was dictated to them by Abdul Latif through Eileen Garrett's mediumship. It soon became a best-seller throughout the English-speaking world, probably because of the accurate diagnoses of medical problems by its alleged spirit author. Medical men to this day still consider *Health, Its Recovery and Maintenance* one of the classic examples of medical books written in the twentieth century—despite the fact that Arthur Conan Doyle, R. H. Saunders, and Eileen J. Garrett were not doctors.

The medium, Arthur Ford, became curious about the identity of his control, Fletcher, and decided to investigate Fletcher's background:

"After Fletcher had come through several times and told where his family lived, I went to look them up. He had been killed in the First World War and his brother gave me a picture of him. We use his middle name of 'Fletcher' since his family, which includes several priests, wouldn't want this name used."[4]

To verify Fletcher's link with the "world beyond," Arthur Ford told of the time "a woman sitter came with a thimble that had belonged to her late grandmother. Now Fletcher gave this woman a message that didn't make any sense to her at all. He said the thimble belonged to a certain woman whom he described and gave an initial of her name. Well, the sitter played the tape of the sitting for her mother who said, 'That's right. That thimble was given to your grandmother by the woman Fletcher described.' "[5]

Don Galloway, author and well-known British psychic, related the following cases of controls establishing their separate identities in this book, *Inevitable Journey*:

"Mrs. [Ena] Twigg has often spoken of her discarnate father working with her as Guide, whilst Mrs. Trixie Allingham works with her husband in Spirit likewise, though with a quite unique form of 'code' of words and

3. Garrett, *Many Voices*, p. 91.
4. *Psychic* magazine, October 1970, pp. 5–6.
5. Ibid., p. 6.

phrases. Midlands medium Mrs. Nella Taylor, widow of a police inspector and . . . very shrewd personality, works with a Guide called Sal, an old Yorkshire gypsy. Although mostly Mrs. Taylor works through ordinary conscious clairvoyance and clairaudience, she is also a trance medium and when Sal speaks through her it is in Yorkshire dialect so broad that even myself, a native Yorkshireman, will have difficulty in immediate understanding. Many modern Yorkshiremen know well enough the difficulty in understanding the very old Yorkshire natives, especially those in the Dales and of the Moors, and it is impossible for Mrs. Taylor to speak in the same dialect in her ordinary conscious state.

"During one of his great many scientific research commissions in America, Douglas Johnson was told by Chang [Johnson's control] that while the medium's own personal radiations were being electronically measured and evaluated with equipment in one laboratory, he, Chang, would prove his independent radiations as a being in his own right, on identical equipment in the laboratory next door—which he promptly did, much to the amazement of the researchers!"

Lenore Piper was considered one of the finest trance mediums of her day. She gave many séances before the Society for Psychical Research, which brought forth "evidential" information from "beyond." I will now quote one of the most interesting examples of one such session:

"In most cases Mrs. Piper would go into a trance with an anonymous sitter. Soon her control (a claimed discarnate who acted as a 'master of ceremonies' for the seance), Phinuit, would appear to bring through the communicators (allegedly dead personalities) who would either speak or write through the medium. Often the information given was highly evidential. On one occasion Oliver Lodge, the famous physicist, sat with Mrs. Piper and gave Phinuit a watch via the entranced Mrs. Piper. Immediately a personality calling himself 'Uncle Jerry' manifested, claiming that the watch had been his. Lodge pressed the communicator for further information about his life and 'Uncle Jerry,' who actually had been an uncle of Lodge's, then gave the names of his companions while alive, some adventures in a place called 'Smith's Field,' almost drowning, killing a cat, owning a snakeskin, and other very trivial memories. Later Lodge contacted still-living relatives and verified as true much of what 'Uncle Jerry' had told him. Mrs. Piper had no way of knowing this information and could only have gotten it through ESP from some source, living or dead."[6]

However, Mrs. Piper was not dealt with kindly in other quarters. C. E. M. Hansel had this to say:

"During her trances she seemed to assume other personalities and speak or write on matters of which she was ignorant after she regained her normal state. Soon a regular 'control' appeared; this was the spirit of a French physician named Phinuit. However, in 1892, Phinuit was largely replaced as 'control' by the spirit of 'G. P.' The initials 'G. P.' were thought to be those of George Pellham, this being a pseudonym for George Pellew, a young English friend of Hodgson [secretary of the American Society for

6. Rogo, *Parapsychology*, p. 264.

Psychical Research] whose sudden death had occurred a few weeks previously.

"The sittings with G. P. as control were reported at length over the next 4 years, and while Mrs. Piper's claim to put herself in contact with spirits was doubted, the findings were long regarded as providing convincing evidence for extrasensory perception. . . .

"Despite the voluminous reports and the eminence of the investigators, it is clear that the case for Mrs. Piper's extrasensory powers rests mainly on the G. P. series. For Phinuit turned out to know little French and less medicine. He explained the former fact by claiming that in life he had lived so long in an English community in Marseilles that he had forgotten his native tongue. Of more likely significance is the fact that Mrs. Piper had only learned a little French at school. Phinuit could give little information regarding his life on earth, which is not surprising as inquiries in France yielded no record of his birth, life or death. On the other hand, he was adept at fishing for information and often contradicted himself. Also, he often displayed signs of temporary deafness when posed with a difficult question. Much of his 'communication' was garbled, incomplete or merely gibberish; but of more concern to the investigators was the fact that he was unable to demonstrate, even to their satisfaction, that he was in direct contact with the spirits of deceased people."[7]

Does the control ever attempt to influence or change the medium's personality or exert its will over that of the medium? Spirit guides, like the people they were, are different from one another in personality and temperament. Some, like Arthur Ford's Fletcher, are more aggressive and outspoken. Fletcher complained that Ford drank and smoked too much and insisted that Ford give up both these vices. It would seem that Fletcher was not entirely happy with his role as Ford's control: "I have to stick with Ford as long as he needs me, but I wish he would die so I can get loose!"[8]

Whereas Arthur Ford's control admonished him for his vices, and attempted to get him to change his habits, Red Cloud apparently treated Estelle Roberts with much kindness and consideration. She claims he never tried to force his will upon her; rather, Red Cloud expected Mrs. Roberts to use the free will that God gave her but that she had to be responsible for her own actions.

How strong are the powers of the control? The following extraordinary experiences related by Estelle Roberts in her autobiography, *Fifty Years A Medium*, perhaps show best the extent of the spirit power:

"As a family we have always been fond of picnics, taking every opportunity to get into open country whenever the weather is fine. I have been on many such excursions with my daughter Eveline, and her husband, Bill, and on two of these there occurred unexpected psychic phenomena which are certainly worthy of record.

7. Hansel, *ESP*, pp. 223, 224.
8. *Psychic* magazine, October 1970, p. 8.

"We had driven to an unspoiled beauty-spot, enclosed on two sides by forest trees. Lunch was over and we were basking in the hot sunshine. Bill, always of an inquiring mind, was quizzing me about Red Cloud and the demonstrations of psychic power he had so often given.

" 'Will he come to you wherever you are?' he asked.

" 'I believe so. He has never failed me yet.'

" 'But out here, amid the trees and sunshine, would he come here?'

" 'I don't see why not.'

" 'Try,' Bill urged.

" 'I'll ask him first,' I said. I did so and Red Cloud willingly agreed to control me.

"From what Bill and Eveline told me afterwards, I gather that Red Cloud took the opportunity to deliver a little lecture on metaphysics to which the two listened with attention, if not always with comprehension.

" 'Does that mean,' Bill interrupted at one juncture, 'that you can control the elements—the wind, the rain, and what have you?'

" 'Watch,' said Red Cloud, 'and I will show you. Turn your eyes to the line of trees that stand behind you. See how still and unmoving they are. No wind disturbs their branches, no breeze rustles their leaves. But if the medium points her hand to the left, see what happens. The wind bends the tree-tops to the left. If she points to the right, they bend to the right. Does that answer your question, my son?'

"It certainly did. As a practical demonstration, it left the pair breathless and they could hardly wait to tell me about it. I came out of trance to hear them both talking at once.

" 'You pointed to the left and all the trees bowed to the left,' they said. 'Then you pointed to the right and they bowed to the right. It was incredible!'

" 'I have no difficulty in believing it,' I told them sincerely."

One could argue that this might have been a case of mass hypnosis; for this reason I have chosen to cite a second example:

"The other instance occurred in late summer towards the end of a six weeks drought. The countryside was tinder dry and common sense should have told us not to smoke while lying comfortably back in the long brown grass. But Eveline is fond of her cigarettes. She relaxed with her eyes closed, a cigarette between her fingers. We must all have drowsed off because the next thing we knew was that the grass was on fire, and the blaze was spreading with alarming speed. We jumped up and tried to stamp out the flames, but it was useless. Fanned by a warm breeze the flames were advancing rapidly towards where our car stood with several others. Parties of nearby picnickers hurriedly collected their belongings, with the drivers running as fast as they could to remove their vehicles from the danger zone.

"Bringing up the rear of my family's retreat, I was suddenly frightened. The fire was clearly out of control and there was nothing we could do but save ourselves and our belongings. But untold damage might result to other people's property as a consequence of our careless action. Desperately I cast about for something we could do that would halt this conflagration. Then I thought of Red Cloud. He had said he was master of the elements; he could help us now. I stopped running and invoked his aid. Then I raised my hand and stood still and silent. And as I did so the flames died down, as if by a miracle. It was a moment I shall never forget however long I live."

Ruby Yeatman had this to say of the above events:

"I knew Mrs. Roberts slightly. She was considered to be a gifted direct-voice medium and a fine clairvoyant. . . . Knowing what extraordinary incidents can, and did, happen in the days of outstanding physical mediumship, I can accept that the instance . . . did actually happen. I can also accept the second incident . . . although it is certainly very unusual . . . and, as she herself called upon Red Cloud for help in an extremity, I also feel sure he would immediately respond and come to her aid. In a much lesser degree I have experienced such spirit help. Nevertheless, I can well understand that a skeptic would find it very hard to accept."

As the reader has seen, the answer to the identity of a control is a riddle yet to be solved. Dr. Lawrence LeShan, noted parapsychologist and author, perhaps sums it up best:

"Very frequently in trance a good medium will demonstrate a very high level of paranormally acquired information. Whether or not it comes from 'spirits'—as most mediums sincerely believe—is anybody's guess."[9]

9. LeShan, *The Medium, the Mystic, and the Physicist*, p. x.

CHAPTER

14

Ghosts and Spirits

It is rumored that in our nation's capital, Washington, D.C., the ghost of Dolley Madison protested vehemently when White House workers attempted to move her rose garden, and the workers immediately abandoned the work.

Many of the First Ladies of the land, such as Grace Coolidge and Eleanor Roosevelt, claimed they felt the presence of Abraham Lincoln.

Harry Truman's book, *Mr. President*, tells of members of the White House Staff, including maids and butlers, who allegedly saw the ghost of Abe Lincoln on many occasions.

Rumors of famous ghosts and spirits are not limited to America and the White House. Many kings, who included among them King Frederick of Denmark and the Swedish King Gustav, were said to have seen ghosts haunting the royal palace in Stockholm. England is rampant with ghosts. For example, the Royal Palace at Hampton Court was the scene of many tragic deaths, especially during the time of King Henry VIII. It is claimed that Anne Bolyn, Henry's second wife, is seen carrying her head under her arm on the anniversary of her beheading, and that Jane Seymour, Henry's third wife who died in childbirth, is heard moaning in the gardens. The most spectacular ghost alleged to be seen is Queen Catherine Howard, Henry's fifth wife, also beheaded, who runs screaming through the so-called Haunting Gallery from the Royal Chapel to the King's Bedroom.

Who or what are ghosts and spirits? Hans Holzer, a well-known ghost hunter, gives the following definition:

"A ghost . . . is the surviving emotional memory of a person who has died in tragedy, suddenly or gradually, and who cannot free himself from the emotional entanglement that binds him to the place of his death. A ghost is usually unaware of his death or that he is what we call a ghost. He is either not aware of the passing of time and the world around him, or is only very dimly aware. In reliving his final agony over and over, a ghost is very much like a psychotic person, removed from reality and unable to free himself."[1]

While there are some who use these terms "ghosts" and "spirits" interchangeably, there are others who do not. Some hold that a spirit is a discarnate (deceased) personality that returns to earth to impart information to the living from the dead. Unlike ghosts, spirits generally have not experienced a tragic or violent death, and therefore are not imbued with an unhappy and unhealthy desire to "haunt" the place of their demise.

Ruby Yeatman explained the difference in more detail:

"A Spirit is the form a human being assumes after the death of the physical body for use in his new (spiritual) environment. Some regard it as the clothing of the soul; others, such as the Theosophists, call it the astral body, or the etheric body. Spiritualists also use this term but I think of the spirit as the body of the Soul, and the Soul as the Divine Spark from the Being Who is at the centre of all. . . .

"A Ghost (Phantom, apparition) is a thought-form imprinted on the atmosphere after a human being or animal has died probably due to the violent, or deep, emotional experience through which the individual has passed. Many people confuse spirits and ghosts, but I feel that if the ghost or spirit talks, touches, or in other definite ways makes himself or herself felt, then this is an emanation of an actual being and not, as it were, a picture on the atmosphere.

"A phantasm, another expression often used, is, on the other hand, the human double or etheric body which may be seen when the individual is still alive on this earth. There are very many accounts of the phantasms of the living and I think that these are a strong link in the evidence for the survival of human personality after death."

In the view of many parapsychologists and researchers, spirits are probably well-adjusted discarnate beings who actually want to help the living whom they contact. Still others view ghosts as imprisoned beings who can only dwell on their own tragic or violent fate.

The consensus of opinion of both psychical researchers and parapsychologists, however, seems to be that the ghost is produced from the mind, whether it be conscious or unconscious, and persists because of past mental actions that result in physical or bodily manifestations. "The ghost is a dramatic memory that can spring into visual existence at certain times and at certain places where an emotional drama has been acted out," explained Andrea Fodor Litkei.

Although it appears that the terms "ghost" and "spirit" overlap, Herbert Greenhouse points out:

"In psychic phenomena a ghost is a manifestation of a dead person that is seen, heard, felt, or sensed (sometimes even smelled) by the living. Parapsychologists and others who investigate ghosts and spirits prefer the term 'apparition' for the visual aspect of a ghost, since they differ on whether the experience is subjective or a ghost is actually present. The terms 'ghost,' 'apparition,' 'spirit,' and 'astral body' overlap: a 'spirit'

1. Holzer, *ESP and You*, p. 181.

is the essence of a deceased person who has survived bodily death; a 'ghost' is the spirit's manifestation to the senses of the living; the 'astral body' is usually the second body of a living person; and 'apparition' may be used for any of these phenomena that are visual."[2]

How and when do ghosts, spirits, etc. appear to the living? In an attempt to help the reader differentiate between ghosts and spirits, I would like to cite three examples. Before doing so, I call the reader's attention to the fact that most psychic researchers contend that the acceptance of a "soul" is a necessary factor in the belief of ghosts. If one can accept the existence of the soul, one can more readily accept the fact that it has suffered sorrow and joy, terror and pain, and other such emotions.

The first example is that of a ghost:

"The spectre of Lady Hamilton of Bothwellhaugh [Scotland] has haunted her ancestral countryside for years. For while her husband was away from home, 'a favourite of the Regent Murray seized his house, turned his wife on a cold night naked into the open fields, where, before morning, she was found raving mad, her infant perishing either by cold or murder.' For years, the ruins of the mansion of Woodhauslee were troubled by the distraught phantom of a woman in white, bearing in her arms her murdered child. And some time after a new mansion had been built, incorporating some of the materials salvaged from the older building, she appeared again."[3]

It seems spirits or spirit apparitions often appear to close relatives at the moment of physical death. According to a number of doctors and nurses, spirits of those already departed also appear to the dying shortly before actual death. The second example is that of a spirit in just such a context. When Eileen Garrett, the famous medium and author, was very young and living in Ireland, she experienced an encounter with an uncle who had just died:

"The door opened quietly and there, by the lamplight from the hall, I saw him [uncle] standing. I was surprised at his appearance of health, for before his death he had seemed feeble and worn. Now he appeared young, erect and strong. I was overjoyed at seeing him, and he showed that he was happy to see me. He asked that I should obey my aunt's wishes whenever possible. He gave me to understand that he realized the difficulties of my present life with her, and predicted that in two years I should be free and would go to study in London. Then, before I had time to ask any questions, the door closed quietly and he was gone.

"My impulse was to run after him, but I found myself rooted to the spot, and gradually it dawned on me that he had gone and I could not reach him. I collapsed in my chair, and on recovering, tried to understand what had happened. When the lamps were lit, and the night came on, I experienced a new peace, for I understood definitely, for the first time, that death is truly a 'coming alive' again, in some place that lies beyond my ordinary seeing. My uncle never visited me again. Nevertheless, I contin-

2. Greenhouse, *The Book of Psychic Knowledge*, p. 172.
3. Ibid., p. 56.

ued to believe that he remained close to me and would be able to hear when I spoke to him."⁴

It would seem this dramatic visitation to Eileen was that of a "friendly spirit." Her uncle appeared to her at a very critical period in her life.

The third example was told to me one Sunday afternoon while visiting with my husband's aunt. In reminiscing over old family pictures, she spoke of a curious happening to my husband when he was a child. The picture which evoked the memory was one of his young cousin, Dorothy, who died of leukemia at the age of eight. My husband was six at the time. The summer before, Dorothy had visited him and his mother and stepfather at their summer home in Greenwood Lake. The two young children spent a great deal of time in one of their "secret places"—Furnace Brook—a marvelous haven of trees and brooks, made to order for playing hide-and-seek. My husband recalled that Dorothy many times wore a favorite white dress there. Four years after she had passed away, when my husband was ten, he went to play one day at the glen in Furnace Brook. His aunt recalled when he arrived back at the house, he was terribly excited and jubilant because he had "seen" Dorothy in her white dress and they had talked and played at Furnace Brook. His aunt conceded that his mother and stepfather were somewhat skeptical, but after the vivid descriptions, his mother became frightened and urged her son not to tell anyone of the incident. My husband said that was the one and only time he ever saw Dorothy after her death and that she never returned again. His aunt felt the appearance might have been in connection with Dorothy's birthday, which, as she recalled, was around that time.

This would not appear to be a case of a child fantasizing over a secret playmate, for Dorothy only returned once—four years after she died. My husband had played at this spot hundreds of times in the four years since her death and at no time had she appeared before. Since hers was a tragic and prolonged dying, perhaps Dorothy wished to return for one more birthday.

What occurs during a haunting? Although ghosts generally haunt places where their violent or tragic death occurred, in a number of cases these phantoms have occupied other spots. Hauntings are almost always linked to death. They consist of various happenings. Sometimes an apparition of the deceased person appears and is "seen" by a living person. At other times, physical phenomena occur, such as movement of furniture, opening of windows, rapping on walls, and even the stopping of a clock. These events generally take place late at night in the house or place where the tragedy occurred. The ghost seems to be reliving the events that led to its demise, and wants to remind the living of those tragic experiences.

Dr. Nandor Fodor, one of the first to pioneer research in hauntings, was an authority on the subject of ghosts, poltergeists, and the like. His daughter, Andrea Fodor Litkei, tells of one of these hauntings:

"Most families go picnicking on weekends when the weather is beautiful. We went 'Ghost Hunting.'

4. Garrett, *Adventures in the Supernormal*, p. 57–58.

"By way of explanation, when I was a child in England, my father was the Director of the International Institute for Psychical Research. It would happen many times that he would be called upon to investigate ghostly hauntings in the stately old mansions of England. More often than not, this would fall upon a weekend and he would tell us to pack up and accompany him.

"I am sure I must have been the envy of all the children in the neighborhood. I was quite unaware of this and took it completely as a matter-of-course that we might bump into an odd ghost or two while spending a pleasant, though not uneventful, two days with various members and friends of the English aristocracy.

"One such weekend we were invited to Raynham Hall, the ancestral home of the Marchioness Townshend of Raynham. . . .

"The prospect of meeting the 'Red Cavalier,' the 'Brown Lady,' 'The Two Ghostly Children' or a restless spaniel called 'Rex' daunted us not at all but rather set a tone of high expectation.

"The 'Red Cavalier,' phantom of the ill-fated Duke of Monmouth, occupied the Monmouth Room, named after him when he slept in it during his stay at the Great House with his royal father.

"The story goes that he was last seen by a relation of the Townshends who woke up to see the Red Cavalier standing at the foot of her bed. . . .

"The Brown Lady who haunted the main staircase of the Hall had actually been 'caught' by two professional photographers, Mr. Indre Shira and Captain Provand, of 49 Dover Street, London. The photograph clearly showed a luminous figure descending the stairs. My father had cross-examined them and since they had withstood it extremely well, it was one of the reasons we were now at Raynham.

"Family legends say that the Brown Lady was Dorothy Walpole, sister of Sir Robert Walpole. Allegedly she was starved to death at Raynham Hall. The best authenticated stories have to do with her appearance in 1849 at a house party given by Lord Charles Townshend who then owned the Great House. A Major and Mrs. Loftus, among numerous other guests, were witnesses to the events.

"The two 'Ghost Children' haunted the Stone Parlor and 'Rex' the ghostly spaniel presumably gamboled with them for company. I believe there were also 'Spectral Gamblers' of the Royal Bedroom. We were told that it was quite usual to find heavy chairs of this room, rearranged the following morning around a large card table. . . .

"We settled down for the night and waited. My mother and I must have fallen asleep when we were awakened by loud noises and creakings overhead, but we were too sleepy to pay much attention. . . .

"Meanwhile, my father, in the Monmouth Room . . . who slept further away . . . told us the next morning that he had found himself in a monster bed in pitch darkness, with the night wearing on endlessly and his nerves tense. . . . He told us he was about to give up his vigil when THUD . . . THUD . . . THUD. . . . Muffled sounds came through the ceiling. He thought it was a man, stepping heavily with boots on. . . .

"Clank . . . clank . . . clank . . . Pots and pans, he told himself.

"Then there was a squeaking, rumbling and screaming as if furniture was being moved on castors. (This must have been the noise that had awakened my mother and myself.)

". . . The Ghosts of Raynham Hall must have had a marvelous time keeping my father awake for the better part of the night."[5]

It may be helpful to explain that the Duke of Monmouth died a very tragic death. He was the illegitimate son of King Charles II of England, born in 1647. Upon the death of his father in 1685, his uncle, James II, became King of England. Monmouth rebelled but was defeated by his uncle's forces at the Battle of Sedgemoor. Two weeks later he was beheaded in the Tower of London.

The Duke of Monmouth is an example of a ghost haunting that began in the seventeenth century. For a more modern haunting we can turn to the somber tragedies that occurred in the house of Beria, Stalin's secret police chief. This story also points up that a period of intense terrorism can have a lasting effect upon a location or house where torture and pain occurred.

"At the height of his power Beria, like Himmler, had personal control of the vast prison camps and forced labour camps in Siberia and elsewhere. Apart from sending men, women and children to their doom, Beria took a sadistic delight in torturing prisoners. . . . His personal residence in Moscow, a huge luxurious mansion guarded by heavy gates, had rows of cubicles or prison cells in the cellar. . . .

"If there is anything in the idea that inanimate objects can be affected by emotion, it should come as no surprise to hear that Beria's home thereafter had the reputation of being haunted. For a long time it stood deserted. Despite the fact that religion and superstition are both discouraged and ridiculed, and that talk of ghosts should have been dismissed by the Communist faithful as superstitious nonsense, there were no immediate takers for the house. The authorities, maintaining a polite silence as to the previous reputation of the house, made it available to the Tunisian diplomatic mission as an embassy. Apart from the offices usual to an embassy . . . there was living accommodation for the Tunisian Ambassador, Ahmed Mestiri, and for Mrs. Mestiri and their two children. Before long the night air in the mansion was rent by fearful shrieks, groans, maniacal laughter, and shouts of derision. One night Madame Mestiri awoke to see a shadowy figure by her bed, warning her to leave, as tragedy hung over the house. And in early 1961 tragedy did strike—at the two-year-old son of M. Ahmed Arfa, a counsellor at the embassy, who fell from a window on the sixth floor and was killed. Not long afterwards M. Chadli Charouche, the Tunisian Consul, skidded near Moscow River while driving home, was flung into the river and drowned."[6]

How can a ghost be released from its haunt? The eminent parapsychologist D. Scott Rogo sympathized with ghosts chained to their areas of haunting and suggested a way of release:

5. Litkei, *ESP*, pp. 83 ff.
6. Bardens, *Ghosts and Hauntings*, p. 57.

"Certain actions, such as prayer or exorcism, carried out in the phantom's behalf or request often terminate the haunting. Such characteristics would imply that the 'ghost' is a conscious, surviving entity."[7]

It might seem odd to end this chapter on the origin of the word "ghost," but following on the heels of the stories just related, it is an interesting note:

"The word 'ghost,' " attests Hans Holzer, "does not carry the imagery of a Halloween fright at all, but merely means 'stranger,' just as the word *hostes*, from which 'ghost' and 'host' are derived, may signify a host, and his guest, in Latin."[8]

7. Rogo, *Parapsychology*, p. 263.
8. Holzer, *ESP and You*, pp. 181–82.

15

Poltergeists

You have just finished reading about ghosts and spirits. Poltergeists are an adjunct to them—or, are they?

"Of all ghostly manifestations guaranteed to make the hackles rise and the hair stand on end, the activities of the poltergeist come high on the list. . . . But when stones appear from nowhere; when furniture is shifted by unseen hands; when objects levitate themselves—not to say when somebody has the physical sensation of being attacked (the terror of the unknown being added to the terror of the tangible), then the abyss of fear is being plumbed. Whole families have been known to flee from their homes at dead of night or in severe winter to escape the depredations of these invisible influences, whatever they are. Clergymen in Britain and elsewhere are constantly being called in to exorcise these noisy 'spirits.' "[1]

Who or what are poltergeists? There are two schools of thought concerning the identity of poltergeists. According to the theory behind the above example, "poltergeist" is a German word meaning noisy or malicious ghost. The accounts of poltergeist happenings have been chronicled throughout history and in all parts of the world. These accounts are not the inventions of the credulous. They are also not merely the imagery of charlatans and fakes. There are many authenticated cases of poltergeist hauntings that have been verified by unquestionable witnesses.

A second theory holds: "The poltergeist phenomenon, then, is usually concerned with the repressed emotions of the child, and with the guilt feelings which often play their own part. Through the centuries, children have played a prominent part in the drama of sorcery, and more than one overimaginative youngster has been arrested and burned with other sorcerers."[2]

This theory was put forth in the early 1920s by Dr. Hewat McKenzie of

1. Bardens, *Ghosts and Hauntings*, p. 90.
2. Garrett, *Many Voices*, p. 76.

the British College of Psychic Science, who believed that the energy of children within a house was the chief factor in producing the poltergeist disturbance. His belief was supported by many studies of children's play patterns examined by Professor William McDougall, also of the College of Psychic Science. McDougall claimed that children had various stages of excitability that changed very rapidly with environmental influences. He felt that children's play methods were not an imitation of adult actions, as was thought, but rather memories of previous cultures from the dawn of time. Dr. McDougall asserted that the poltergeist manifestations were a necessary working through of these past memories by the children in order to fit them for the adult life they faced.

The concept was taken a degree further by the eminent parapsychologist and psychoanalyst Dr. Nandor Fodor, who, in his controversial book, *On the Trail of the Poltergeist*, to which Sigmund Freud wrote the preface, propounded the theory that suppressed sexual energy or creative energy was the probable cause for poltergeist manifestations.

Andrea Fodor Litkei, the late doctor's daughter, recalled the furor her father's book caused in certain circles:

"In the 1930s, poltergeists were considered to be noisy ghosts, departed spirits, discarnate entities or what have you and when, in 1938, he [Dr. Fodor] finished the controversial manuscript and made history with it with Freud, the uproar was tremendous; that Dr. Fodor's theory that such phenomena could be the unconscious compliance of an existing situation, that there could be any sexual outlet or it could be a bundle of repressions, was absolutely flabbergasting. All the mediums were extremely upset and he was considered as exposing and being against what then was known as spiritualism and not parapsychology."

Authors Dennis Bardens and Raymond Bayless are strong advocates of the first theory, that poltergeists are a mischievous and sometimes malignant force or spirit. They assert that the poltergeist enjoys throwing stones, lifting objects, smashing glasses and the like. Further, they quote examples from earliest time to the present of poltergeist activity: "The poltergeist is as old as history. Cases were recorded in Ancient Egypt, Greece and Rome" wrote Bayless in *The Enigma of the Poltergeist*. "Famed disturbances were noted during the Middle Ages, the Renaissance, etc. and are equally active today. Hauntings following the Colonists to the New World and current cases are being investigated now in the interests of science."

"Consider, for instance," adds Bardens, "how extraordinarily persistent are reports of unexplained showers of stones. In A.D. 530, according to Cyprian's *Life of St. Caesarius of Arles*, one reads that Deacon Helpidius, physician to King Theodoric, was troubled in his house by noisy spirits and by showers of stones actually *inside* the house. Showers of stones afflicted the house of Bishop Hugh of Maus in 1138. In 1170, the hermitage of poor St. Godric was hit by showers of stones. The Cieza de Leon (1549) describes how, during his conversion to Christianity, the Cacique of Pirza, in Popyou, was bombarded by a hail of stones appearing from out of the air, while Mr. Dennys in *Folk Lore of China*, published 1876, tells of a Chinese householder who fled from his home to a temple for refuge from Poltergeists which threw crockery about and made life intolerable by their heavy footfalls."[3]

And in the twentieth century, these poltergeist happenings were recorded: "In a school near Richardton, Canada, in April, 1944, lumps of coal jumped out of a pail like Mexican jumping beans; in July, 1935, a servant girl in Prague was astounded to find that as she walked towards a door it would automatically open before she reached it, and that potatoes in a cellar rolled towards her; in South Africa (Cape Town), in 1932, a house in Maitland, a suburb, was haunted by a poltergeist able to cause spontaneous conflagration. Papers allowed to flutter to the ground would burst into flames. So, too, did clothing locked safely away in cupboards. . . . It will be enough to say that the behaviour and doings of poltergeists constitute a distinct 'branch' of haunting."[4]

Fires seem to be a major poltergeist activity, occurring almost as frequently as showers of stones and rocks:

"Mysterious fires occur during poltergeist infestations. Numerous fires plagued a boy in British Guiana [in 1960] and a religious service or exorcism proved ineffectual. A home in Texas [Houston] became the scene of repeated fires and other violent phenomena. A complex case in Canada [Quebec Province] offered extremely violent effects, including several fires, and a very human-like voice of the invading poltergeist was clearly heard."[5]

I have described at some length the school of thought that maintains poltergeists are noisy ghosts or spirits. To recap, this theory holds that poltergeists have been rampant for centuries and that they generally conform to the following description: noises in empty rooms, furniture moving about, raps or knocks on doors or walls, shattered china or crockery, unexplained fires, and rocks and stones flying through the air.

The advocates of this school, believing that poltergeists are ghosts, contest the hypothesis of some psychoanalysts and psychiatrists that the basis of poltergeist manifestations is usually disturbances that occur in homes where one or more adolescents are going through puberty. Because there are probably few homes where puberty has not occurred, one would contend that poltergeists should be the rule rather than the exception. And yet, poltergeist activity is rare indeed.

The second school of thought—holding the view that the energy of children within a house is the chief factor in producing the poltergeist disturbance—seems to be upheld by modern psychology. When a poltergeist manifests itself, either a parapsychologist or psychoanalyst is called in to investigate the noisy activity. One of the first questions asked is "Is there a child twelve or thirteen years old living in the house?" Once a child is produced, a skilled analyst will quickly get to the root of the poltergeist problem. The child needs attention, and in order to attract the attention of his peers and the adults around him, he directs his discontent into seemingly violent happenings.

3. Bardens, *Ghosts and Hauntings*, p. 91.
4. Ibid., p. 44.
5. Bayless, *The Enigma of the Poltergeist*, p. 103.

A chief exponent of this viewpoint, Dr. Hewat McKenzie, thought that children in puberty were at the base of poltergeist activity. However, he also thought that there could be a combination of pubic energy with ghostly manifestations:

". . . he [Hewat McKenzie] also believed that the loose energy or 'imprisoned ghost' could be drawing attention to some hidden conflict in the home. That is to say, the essence of a person who had departed this life could affect the actions of those remaining in the flesh, and the young child could very well obey this influence. Energy was the servant; spirit and mind the master."[6]

Eileen Garrett, who was a student of Dr. McKenzie's and later worked with him on psychic experiments, cited an example of such a "haunting" which corroborates Dr. McKenzie's views:

"McKenzie was asked to go back again. It seems that after we had been ordered out, many strange things happened; ominous rattles, breakages, movements of objects, bedclothes stripped off the boys, and so on. The farmer at first thought the boys were playing pranks; but he was now thoroughly frightened and said he knew 'the goblins' were trying to get him. He had become convinced that he was in the power of an evil force, and the woman also was thoroughly frightened. When we went back, I [Mrs. Garrett] was permitted to sit down, and I went into a condition of trance. McKenzie entered into conversation with Uvani [Eileen's control], who revealed that the real mother was present. She was intent on freeing her children, and indicated there was enough money to get them into good schools. . . . Here, at least, was a 'departed' personality at work. Here, also, was a conflict and anxiety about the children, the loss of the mother, the intrusion of the other woman, the greed of the father, the suppressions —all these provided the ingredients for a typical poltergeist case."[7]

Eileen told of another experience in which she herself was a participant:

"Finally, I was myself able one evening to sit by the bedside of Gwilliam, the little fellow, who fortunately appeared to like me. While he was dozing, I actually saw the bed covers being removed, as though rough hands had torn them away. In falling to the ground, they appeared to be suspended for a moment by some invisible force. There was a 'tearing' sound in the room, but on examination nothing had been damaged.

"This was the first time I was able to witness actual phenomena happening. Often these things take place in the twinkling of an eye, and usually there are none present as actual witnesses. I saw this happen on two separate occasions in one night and felt an uncomfortable presence in the room."[8]

These two examples would seem to indicate that Dr. McKenzie might have been on an interesting trail when he stated that poltergeists generally involved children at puberty. The two examples also appear to strengthen his argument that "something else"—a spirit personality concerned with the welfare of the child or children involved—could be an added ingredient.

6. Garrett, *Many Voices*, p. 76.
7. Ibid., pp. 79–80.
8. Ibid., p. 89.

Before ending this chapter, let's look closer at Dr. Nandor Fodor's theories of poltergeists and repressed sexual activity. In an interview, his daughter, Andrea Litkei, recalled his philosophy on poltergeists:

"Now, if I try to recall to the best of my abilities some of his [Dr. Fodor's] ideas on the mechanics of poltergeist activities, I would say that the actual mechanics really is the central mystery. It is not enough to say . . . that the poltergeist is a bundle of projected repressions. He said we should want to answer as to how the projection takes place. What is the nature of the energy involved? Is it muscular? This is providing his hypothesis is correct that it is suppressed sexual energy, or creative energy for that matter. Is it muscular, nervous, electric, or electronic? How does it work? We do not know. Therefore, the best we can do is to take a speculative approach.

"He [Dr. Fodor] called the poltergeist manifestation a result of somatic and psychic dissociation. Somatic dissociation is something new. It has never been postulated before. It means that the human body is capable of releasing energy in a manner similar to atomic bombardments. The electron shot out of its orbit around the proton is like a bolt of lightning. It can be photographed streaking through the air in a cloud chamber. It is purely mechanical energy. The atom as such has no power to impart direction to it. A human being has. It appears that under strong emotions not only does such a discharge, happily without chain reaction, take place, but that the energy released is under control. A poltergeist-thrown object can travel slowly or fast. It can change course as if part of the psyche of the projector would travel with it, as if the somatic dissociation that releases it were not free from mental control. But even this hypothesis leaves a great deal unexplained."

In this chapter, I have tried to present fairly the different views on the subject of poltergeists: (1) A poltergeist is a ghost or spirit that creates havoc and mayhem. This view apparently looks upon the poltergeist as a discarnate spirit that haunts the living for purely mischievous purposes. (2) The poltergeist is the physical reaction of children going through puberty, giving off energy based on the sexual change. According to this thesis, poltergeist manifestations almost always take place when a twelve- or thirteen-year-old child is present. (3) A purely psychoanalytical view sees a poltergeist manifestation as an expression of a sexual change, of sexual repression, or a sexual energy explosion. (4) A further theory expressed by some psychic researchers holds that poltergeist activity may be a manifestation of PK.

These are the viewpoints expressed by some of the foremost authorities in the field of psychic phenomena, and in particular of those investigating poltergeist activity.

Sittings and Séances

A séance cannot be held with just two people.
A Sitting can be—and most sittings are.

I was first made aware of sittings during a visit to the College of Psychic Studies in London. It was here that I first met Bo-Goran Sleeman, with whom I had a sitting. Later, my husband also had a sitting with Bo-Goran.

I recall climbing a flight of stairs to the second floor of the college and being ushered into a quiet little room. I sat down, not knowing what to expect. Bo-Goran was a very intriguing man, with piercing eyes, who kept rubbing his hands together, almost in a semitrance, as if reaching for something. In an instant, he turned to me and exclaimed that there were tremendous psychic forces spinning around the room, and that he felt I had an enormous amount of psychic ability. For the balance of our time together Bo-Goran described the problems in my life, my illnesses, and where he thought my place of residence would ultimately be.

The sitting with my husband was more dramatic. Bo-Goran first told my husband that standing next to him was a young girl of eighteen, who claimed her name was Violet. My husband's mother had died sixteen years earlier. Her name was Claire Veronica, but she had always wished to be called Violet, which was her favorite color and flower. Bo-Goran continued: "Violet says she will protect you from harm." Later in the sitting my husband was told that a man named Ralph was trying to communicate. Ralph was asking for my husband's forgiveness, Bo-Goran stated, and asked that a message be conveyed to his wife and children. What made this sitting particularly interesting was that my husband had an uncle named Ralph, who had died six years previously. Further, my husband and his Uncle Ralph had not spoken to each other for many years prior to his death, because of a family quarrel. Just before his death, he contacted my husband and tried to make amends for the lost years but died before the situation could be rectified. When my husband delivered the message to Ralph's daughter, she considered it evidential.

The above instances are cited to show what can take place at a sitting. For a more comprehensive understanding of sittings, Paul Beard, president of the College of Psychic Studies, supplied the following answers to my inquiries:

What exactly is a sitting? If one came to the college and knew nothing of mediums, what could one expect to happen at a sitting? How long does a sitting usually last? "If one came to the college and knew nothing of mediums, one would not expect to be able to receive as good an interview [sitting] as would a more experienced person. The sitter can very often interfere with the mediumistic flow simply because they do not know how to conduct themselves at an interview. Broadly speaking, the conduct of the sitting should be left to the medium. In other words, the medium must be allowed to tell her own story and a sitter's part should be limited as far as possible to giving confirmation, if asked to do so, or to ask questions if given the opportunity. It is hoped within the next year to publish a booklet giving advice to novices on how to sit with sensitives. An hour is usually allowed for a sitting but the effective part of it may be only a part of such a period and some mediums have said all that they can say within twenty minutes or thirty minutes."

The booklet referred to above, *Hints on Consulting a Sensitive*, by Paul Beard, is now available at a nominal charge and may be obtained by writing to the College of Psychic Studies, 16 Queensberry Place, London S. W. 7, England.

What is generally charged for a sitting? Are there sittings in the United States comparable to those given at the college? "Sensitives fix their own fees at the college and the college adds a small service charge as a contribution towards the overhead, but never enough to cover it. Therefore, in the long run, the college depends, and is likely always to have to depend, on legacies and donations in order to continue to exist. An average fee for an interview with a sensitive these days [1976] is around £4 sterling. No doubt there are sittings and interviews in the United States in a general way comparable to those given at the College, but I think it is generally accepted that on the whole the standard is higher in England, whether at the College or elsewhere. Not so much attention is given in England to the health and general financial well-being of the client, and more to attempted communication with discarnate persons."

When and why did the college initiate the program of mediums and sittings? At the college, is training given to prospective mediums? "The College was founded in 1884 and it has always been its policy and purpose to provide for investigation into the evidence which can be provided by mediums and sensitives, but always from an open-ended point of view. Essentially the enquirer is left to form his own conclusions and is certainly never at any time required to hold any particular beliefs in order to be able to be a member of the College. The College sponsors training of prospective mediums. The art of mediumship is a very difficult one calling for a number of different qualities from the trainee, in addition to psychic sensitivity as such. The failure rate is necessarily very high."

What goes on at a sitting? After many discussions and much correspondence with those in the field of psychic studies, it would appear that: (1) The sensitive generally conducts the sitting on a one-to-one discussion basis, without going into trance. (2) During the sitting, some sensitives claim to see discarnate beings hovering around the sitter. (3) Some sensitives state they hear voices and convey messages to the sitter from the "voices." (4) Still other sensitives hold objects and receive impressions from handling them. (5) Some sensitives practice automatic writing. This is performed with pencil and paper or with a ouija board. Presumed messages are received from discarnate spirits for the sitter. Automatic writing is accomplished without going into trance. (More about automatic writing in a later chapter.) (6) On rare occasions, a sitter may have the unique and dramatic experience of having a sitting with a trance medium. While in trance the medium undergoes a personality change—reflected in voice and demeanor—which is interpreted as being that of the control, or guide. The controls assert they are voices of discarnate spirits who want to communicate through the medium to the sitter. (7) On even rarer occasions, a further transformation in the trance medium takes place. The control steps aside and the departed soul speaks directly in its *own* voice to the sitter through the trance medium.

With so many individuals having "passed over" throughout the world, why is it that only some are able to contact specific individuals here? Don't all people, regardless of where they died, land in the same place and want to contact specific persons living? Is there some sort of wait-your-turn system before contact with the living can be made? "Communication between this world and the next is much more difficult than many people realise," Ruby Yeatman wrote in answer to my question. "Considering all the difficulties, it is remarkable that we get as much as we do. Many communicators have stressed, when speaking through a medium, the difficulty they encounter in trying to get through exactly what they want to say. Remember there are usually 3 or 4 individuals taking part in a sitting, i.e. the sitter, the medium, the medium's Control, and the Communicator. The medium has to be able to receive the message from the Control (if a trance medium). The Control has to understand exactly what the Communicator wishes to convey and then the Control has to find the right expression in the medium's mind or consciousness to express the message or description. In automatic writing, the sensitive has to be wary in relation to his own subconscious mind, which may intrude and cause distortion. When the conscious mind is quiescent, it is amazing what will well up from the unconscious—very good stuff too.

"Referring to the difficulties encountered, the Rev. Drayton Thomas' father, when communicating with him through the mediumship of Mrs.

Osborne Leonard (the famous British medium) stressed more than once how difficult he found it to convey his exact meaning; it was as though he had to get through a fog, and often Feda, the Control, did not understand him correctly. Sir William Barrett, when speaking to Lady Barrett, told her that it was easier for him to talk of his scientific work than to say, 'I am Will.' Another communicator, a great scholar, in a little book entitled 'Letters From the Other Side' said he found it easier to speak of his beautiful daughter than to get her name through. This Communicator was very successful in answering questions of various kinds.

"Doubtless people of various nationalities might and do wish to get into touch with their friends left over here, but it is possible that beliefs they have held, and in which they have been nurtured, might prevent them from making the attempt. Also, bear in mind that there do not appear to be a great number of human beings suitable to act as 'go-betweens' or instruments between this world and the next."

Might one who has passed over in one country contact someone in another country by mistake? How are the routes of communications established? Is it similar to a long-distance telephone call, with the medium acting as the telephone operator to assure reaching the proper country and person? If so, who acts as the "medium" on the other side for those who have passed over? (Asked of Ruby Yeatman.)

"This has been partially answered above. One hoping and wishing to communicate would need to find a suitable instrument here on earth, and we understand such an instrument is found by the light surrounding him or her. Each sensitive, or medium, usually attracts one or more dedicated workers in the Unseen who make a special point of caring for their instrument and it is that one, the Control, or Guide, of the medium, who will help a particular communicator to get his messages through to the sitter. In certain instances, the Control will stand aside and allow the particular communicator to give his own message; that is known as direct control."

For how long can those who have passed over hope to contact persons here? "There is no time limit, as it were, to communication so long as the spirit remains within the orbit of the earth," explained Ruby Yeatman, "but after what is called 'the second death' there is no communication, except perhaps by influence filtering down. This is shown, I think, fairly clearly in Geraldine Cummins' book 'The Scripts of Cleophas,' where Cleophas, long dead, communicates scripts through the hand of Miss Cummins."

What can living people hope to learn from departed spirits when they do communicate with them successfully? Is it wise for the ordinary person to try to communicate with a departed spirit? Is it wise to ask for everyday advice? Could not such communication in a sitting be dangerous, i.e., a dependency on the spirits to guide one's everyday actions? Ruby Yeatman replied:

"Bearing in mind that the chief purpose of Spiritualism is to prove the continuity of life after death and to offer evidence of personal identity, when these facts have been established to the satisfaction of the enquirer [sitter], then if the Communicator and Enquirer are intelligent people interested in work other than messages for comfort or of a personal nature, it is possible for the Enquirer to receive information and knowledge on many subjects, including life and work in the spiritual body and/or explanations, or answers to questions, concerned with ethical or philosophical matters, possibly also matters of a scientific nature but this would depend upon the qualities of both Communicator and Enquirer, and the quality of the mediumship itself. I would refer you to some of the books written by the late Rev. C. Drayton Thomas, such as 'Life Beyond Death with Evidence,' 'Precognition and Human Survival' and many others. For outstanding quality of communications, such as I believe have not since been equalled, I would recommend reading the book by Dr. Walter Franklin Prince on 'The Case of Patience Worth.'

"It is certainly most unwise for any Enquirer to seek sittings with mediums for the sole purpose of obtaining advice as to his daily life or affairs. Such a motive is not encouraged by genuine Controls or Communicators who deprecate any lack of self reliance; sooner or later such Enquirers would meet with disappointment or contradictory statements, or with some sensitives they simply receive back their own desires psychically 'picked up' by the sensitive—here is one of the psychological aspects of mediumship.

"This does not discount the fact that often good advice is proffered *spontaneously* by a Control, or friend, through a medium, which can be given serious consideration and acted upon but always any advice given by or through a medium should be submitted to one's own intuitive and reasoning power before being accepted.

"Continued reliance upon statements made by mediums does constitute a danger and is something that should be discouraged. In the study of this subject, as in all others, common sense should be observed. Friends who have passed over only know a little more than we do (as a rule), can only see a little way ahead and can make mistakes both as regards time and in trying to convey what they really want to say. Communication is far from easy and some never do manage it."

Now, on to a séance.

What is a séance? What conditions are necessary to a séance? Never having participated in a séance myself, I gathered the following information in research and present it only to provide you with some insight as to what might possibly happen at a séance. Most séances are conducted in the presence of a physical medium. A séance also includes a circle of people, the sitters, whose presence is supposed to enhance the psychic forces of the medium. In serious séance attempts, a meticulous search is made of the medium and the room in which the séance is held in order to preclude fraud. Generally, doors and windows are locked after the medium enters the séance room. The séance is usually held in either total darkness or semidarkness.

What are some things one might witness at a séance? VOICE OR TRUMPET SPEAKING: This involves a discarnate spirit attempting to speak directly to the sitters. Apparently the use of the trumpet is to enhance the faintness of the voices. The soft and often indistinct sounds of these so-called spirit messages are therefore conducted through the trumpet in an attempt to increase sound and clarity. MATERIALIZATION: This occurs in a darkened room. It has been claimed that human forms or parts of human forms, such as hands, face, or head, materialize before the sitters. Such materializations are supposed to represent people who have died and who are trying to contact one of the sitters. TELEKINESIS, OR MOVING OF OBJECTS: This includes the lifting of tables, chairs floating through the air, glasses being smashed against the wall, all without normal physical movement or aid from the sitters or the medium. At times, apports (objects such as flowers or fruit) appear in the séance room apparently by paranormal means. TABLE TURNING AND TABLE TILTING: This psychic phenomenon is similar to automatic writing and ouija-board readings. The hands of the medium and the sitters are placed on the table. A question is asked and purportedly a discarnate being answered by turning or tilting the table.

Do these manifestations occur through paranormal means? If not, why do people attend séances? Sadly, in many instances, fraud has been discovered. If you do have any plan to attend a séance, it is probably best to do so with an open mind—not everything can be taken at face value.

Most people express the desire to attend a séance for a variety of reasons. The main one seems to be to receive messages of comfort from loved ones who have died. Whatever the reason, I would urge that caution be exercised in attending a séance. You might heed these words of Ruby Yeatman:

"As regards day to day affairs, certainly Eileen Garrett gave wise advice and opinion for one should never act blindly upon information or advice given from the Unseen, (or by mediums) or seeping into one's own consciousness, without submitting all such to reason and commonsense. . . . Each individual has to decide for himself what course to take."

It would be convenient if we could close this chapter with a description of what "life" is like for those who passed over, but we can't. There is still not enough "evidence" to say for sure. But we do know that we have merely scratched the surface that separates the here from the hereafter. Perhaps Ruby Yeatman's analogy of the two worlds is a more fitting conclusion:

"Please bear in mind that all accounts and descriptions regarding life in the next world do but touch the fringe of the subject. It seems to me that life There is, for instance, as different from life Here as is the life of the caterpillar from that of the butterfly. How could the wisest caterpillar envisage his life as a butterfly? Yet, that is what he will become."

PART IV

The Trail Leads to Life After Life

When people say they believe in survival of life, what do they mean? Dr. Raynor C. Johnson meant he would discard his earthly body and use another "vehicle" which he already possessed—the soul. Paul Beard believes that a spirit capable of existing without a physical body lives on after life as a subtle manifestation of its former self. Eileen J. Garrett was certain there was no end of life. She believed the consciousness lives on in the "eternal universe of mind."

I always wondered why it was important to the living that life existed after life. I asked Ruby Yeatman many questions on this subject. She felt it was important to the living to give reassurance of continued existence. This knowledge could prevent suicide, help alleviate the grief of those who have lost loved ones, and give reason to humanistic principles of spiritual values beyond mere physical being. Ruby claimed it was important for man to study the question of survival so he could learn more about his entire personality—physically and spiritually, now and beyond.

But how to prove life after death? What do the experts consider evidence of survival of life? Paul Beard's principal answer was: ". . . deliberate and sustained two-way conversation, with opportunities for question and answer. We want to establish whether the personality of a dead person can contact us in its fullness, and continue to do so." Thus, Paul is not particularly interested in short mediumistic communications dealing with trivia. He is primarily interested in long conversations of a question-and-answer nature. Ruby Yeatman's idea of evidence of survival consists of information received through a medium which not only was beyond the medium's knowledge but would reflect the "tricks of the personality of the departed person." She also claims the presence of the discarnate should be sensed in some way—not necessarily sighted.

Much of the evidence of survival of life has been gathered by automatic writing—written messages produced unconsciously by mediums or sensitives from outside or discarnate sources. Authors such as Nostradamus, William Blake, Robert Louis Stevenson, and André Breton have employed it to produce books. Artists such as Matisse, Picasso, and Derain experimented with "automatic painting" in the 1920s. Eileen J. Garrett used it in conjunction with medical doctors to ascertain illnesses and cures of various patients. On the whole, psychics and parapsychologists accept automatic writing as a fact. The controversy is in determining where the writing is coming from.

Most automatic writers and mediums claim it's from the spiritual world. Many parapsychologists feel it is being drawn from the unconscious of the medium or automatist. Others assert the medium is receiving telepathic messages from another living being. Naturally, if the mediums are correct and automatic writing comes from discarnate spirits, it would be strong evidence in support of survival of life.

Another indication of survival of life is reincarnation—the transmigration of souls. This theory has deep religious roots that go back to the beginning of human history. Egyptians, Greeks, Druids, Jews, Hindus, and Buddhists all espoused it. Simply stated, reincarnation means the survival of the soul after the death of the body—and its occupation of another living body some time afterward. Although some people believe the soul has to wait a period of time before "taking on flesh again," most reincarnationists assert the soul transmigrates immediately. In its broadest sense, reincarnation means "to be born again"—to have a chance to learn from past mistakes and to become wholesome through experience and evolution.

These are some of the things we intend to touch upon in this, the final and most controversial part of the book.

CHAPTER

17

Survival After Life

Dr. Raynor C. Johnson, author of many important books in the fields of parapsychology and physics, tells us what he believes survival of death means:

"When I refer to my survival of death, I mean merely that I shall some day discard as no longer serviceable this outer-most vehicle or instrument. Another vehicle or instrument of myself, which I at present possess but do not consciously use, then becomes my outer or objective expression on a level of reality to which it inherently belongs. Glimpses of its existence are found in accounts of out-of-body experiences."[1]

By "out-of-body" experiences, Dr. Johnson is referring to the experiences of some people who claim that they leave their body and travel. This is also known as astral projection. Many persons have described seeing their body in bed fast asleep while they hovered above watching.

Dr. Alex Tanous, well-known psychic, explains that the terms "out-of-body experiences" and "astral projection" are used interchangeably, both indicating a phenomenon in which the "traveler" is able to view events going on at places far from where his body is. In most cases, according to Dr. Tanous, observers would have to also be psychic in order to see him. In the situation of "bilocation," (being two places at once), here the observers—whether psychic or not—can see the "traveler," but the "traveler" may or may not see them. In his book Beyond Coincidence, Tanous defines an out-of-body experience as one "in which some relatively intangible part of a person leaves his body and returns," and "astral projection" as "the casting out and later retrieval of one's 'astral body,' a kind of energy or spirit entity . . ."

In describing his own out-of-body experiences (known as OBEs in psychic circles), Alex Tanous tells of early tests conducted with him by Dr. Karlis Osis, director of the American Society for Psychical Research, which had long been interested in the question of whether some part of the human personality is able to operate outside the living body and might

1. Johnson, Psychical Research, p. 145.

continue to do so after death. An initial task for Alex was to attempt to leave his body while hundreds of miles away and project himself in some way into Dr. Osis' office to view different objects placed on a table there for testing purposes. In each of five trials, Alex—while in Maine—was able to accurately describe the objects, colors and events taking place in Dr. Osis' office in New York.

Later, more intensive OBE experiments were undertaken in which Tanous was asked if he could take a trip out of body and locate a former ASPR researcher now living in California, which he agreed to try. Alex states he twice left his body, directing himself towards California. He then clearly saw the woman researcher, described the clothing she was wearing at the time, and stated she was not living in an ordinary house, but in a houseboat. Later, it was verified that his description of the houseboat, the clothing worn when he "saw" the woman, and other details about the location off the California coast were all correct.

Dr. Tanous realizes how difficult it may be for the average person to accept the idea that someone can leave his body, go elsewhere and observe things, and then return without ever having moved physically. However, he asserts, it is possible.

The possibilities of this phenomenon are enormous for mankind, Dr. Tanous believes: "If a living man is able to detach part of himself, send it elsewhere, then retrieve it, might not a dying man detach part of himself and not retrieve it, leaving that part to survive him after death? Does such a thing happen automatically after death?"[2]

Alex Tanous is many men—a psychic, author, national lecturer and panelist, as well as being a Doctor of Divinity. He also teaches parapsychology at the University of Maine. In a recent interview, he explained that in his college course, he teaches the philosophy and common sense of parapsychology. When asked what the purpose of teaching OBEs was, Dr. Tanous stated there were several reasons: "One is if you are really tired and you can do an OBE, you come back very rested. Another is that the OBE is to set one at ease if the experience happens to them spontaneously. A very important reason is so that one may begin to experience something about life after death. An out-of-body experience is a tangible expression to the person experiencing it that there is survival." Once his students have experienced an OBE, "they are able to understand it, and that this entity as it stands alone while they are still living, has a function, and then there is no reason for that entity to die. It is survival of man which is expressed in the out-of-body experience and therefore by the actual experiencing of it, they overcome the fear of death and are no longer afraid of it."

What does an "out-of-body experience" feel like and how is it done? Alex Tanous tells us how he goes about it: "I find myself a comfortable position in a quiet room, empty my mind of extraneous thoughts and say to myself, 'Mind, leave my body now. Go to New York. Enter Dr. Osis' office' (for example). Again and again, I repeat these phrases to myself, slowly, silently, thinking about nothing else. At a certain point, I find that I

2. Tanous with Ardman, *Beyond Coincidence*, p. 114.

am without a body. I consist of a large spot of light, of consciousness, which gradually gets smaller and more concentrated.

"Time then seems to stop for a moment and I am aware of an image. The image lasts for an indeterminate length of time, then disappears. Then I am conscious only of a spot of light. I have no other words to describe the experience. . . .

"After a while, quite automatically, quite beyond my control, I return. I would love to remain outside of my body, for it is very pleasant indeed, but I have no say in the matter. Before I can think about it, I am back, almost as if I have awoken.

"I know it sounds simple—maybe too simple. When the procedure works, it is simple. When it doesn't it is impossible."[3]

Are there common deathbed experiences or do we each go in our own way? You have probably read accounts of people on their deathbed—or those who almost died but were brought back—having strange visions. The patients often claim to have seen apparitions of those already dead (a close relative, friend, or stranger) who had come to assist them through the death experience.

The following summaries by D. Scott Rogo were culled from a study published as a monograph, *Deathbed Observations by Physicians and Nurses,* by Dr. Karlis Osis, former head of the division of research at the Parapsychology Foundation and currently research director of the American Society for Psychical Research:

"1. The dying often exhibit a period of exaltation shortly before death. This state is not due to the nature of the disease, education level, or sex, and only mildly to the patient's belief concerning survival of death.

"2. The dying do have visual experiences near death enormously above the rate of visions or hallucinations observed by a normal population.

"3. These visions, often of apparitions, occurred for the most part while the patient was in clear consciousness, not sedated, and were seen most commonly between one hour to one day before death.

"4. These visions are most often of the dead, though other figures are seen.

"5. Half of the percipients stated that the apparitions were going to take them into death."[4]

In a recent discussion with Dr. Osis, he brought us up to date in his findings: "Deathbed visions were not caused by disturbed brain processes, high temperature, morphine or other medical reasons. Were they true glimpses of the beyond? A lingering doubt remained; they could be explained as a playback of religious beliefs. The dying patient might just imagine that he sees messengers from afterlife while actually he is reproducing old Bible stories."

Dr. Osis told of a trip he took to India to answer this question, "A new study was conducted where 442 deathbed visions of Americans were compared with 435 of Indian patients. Would Indians *see* the imagery of the

3. Ibid., p. 126.
4. Rogo, *Parapsychology*, p. 274.

Veda while Americans see images out of the Bible? No, deathbed visions were similar in both cultures. Indians and Americans alike seem to see what in reality is out there rather than fantasize stories of their scriptures." This is described in more detail in Dr. Osis' newest work entitled *What They Saw at The Hour of Death.*

If man is capable of experiencing communication with a living mind, can he similarly be in contact with the "minds" of those already dead? It has been shown in the chapter "Mediums and Sensitives" that allegedly discarnate spirits—i.e. departed souls—were capable of practicing telepathy and precognition, among other ESP talents. If this be true, then why cannot the mind refocus from the present world to the world beyond? If the mind is capable of ESP while alive, and one assumes that some semblance of the mind lives on after death, then why not a mind capable of ESP after death as well as before?

But if, upon physical death, the brain deteriorates and there is no more "mind" as we know it, then with what type of energy could one communicate after death? Eileen J. Garrett answers from the medium's standpoint:

"Long reflection on these problems leads me to suggest that perhaps an entity capable of existing without body may escape and live in some subtle manifestation of energy related to air as air is related to matter; and after death of the body, it may continue to exist and appear as a dim expression of its onetime more robust self—a ghost of itself able to communicate with mortals through the perceptive feelings of one like myself."[5]

Is dying the end of life? Eileen Garrett believed there is no ending to life and shares a poignant moment:

"I feel, as I lie in bed awaiting the command to 'give up' or 'carry on,' that there is a plan. Personality or individuality then appears to be no more than a biological device which serves evolution. A consciousness or something greater takes hold. I have arguments with myself as to what the act of dying means. In my innermost and most revealing moments, I cannot find any need to hear of the conviction of others, nor do I feel myself separated from the life of nature, that energy which determines the motions of the electrons and the heavenly bodies. One thing is certain: There is no ending to life, animate or inanimate, or to the endless ordered rhythm of the universe."[6]

Where does one begin in exploring the issue of survival of death? Paul Beard suggests that those who are interested "will find it worth asking what—assuming that it were possible for it to be provided—he would accept as valid evidence of survival. Having done this—and it is indeed no easy task—a further question then needs to be asked immediately. If this evidence were to come to him, would he then find that he would after all feel it necessary to change his ground, and decide he must ask for some further evidence still? And if he were given this further evidence, would he

5. Garrett, *Many Voices,* p. 229.
6. Ibid., p. 181.

provide still further demands to be met? If so, is it because he is already committed to a view of life in which survival is deemed impossible, and his enquiry is therefore, however subtly, being prejudged?"[7]

In short, we must keep an open mind.

The more I thought about survival after life, the more questions arose that needed answering. I presented some of them to Ruby Yeatman for her wise counsel:

What is considered evidence of survival? "I quote Mercy Phillimore, at one time Secretary of the London Spiritualist Alliance, the leading Spiritualist Society: 'All personal information that comes from a particular spirit through a medium to a sitter who is without knowledge of it is evidence to identity if on subsequent enquiry it is found to be true. On the strength of this good evidence we are justified in believing in the evidential value of a mass of true information which is given concerning a communicator and which is known to the sitter.' Much information may be given which will bear the stamp of a mind other than that of the medium in operation, together with tricks of the personality of the departed person and above all the sense of the actual presence of another being, unseen but felt perhaps in an indefinable manner."

Paul Beard takes this a step further:

"We seek evidence of *identity*. We also ask of the facts that they shall not be merely random, vague, and without meaning and coherence; we require them to show evidence of *purpose*. With mediumistic communications, then, we are no longer concerned with the brief telepathic impact, but with deliberate and sustained two-way conversation, with opportunities for question and answer. We want to establish whether the personality of a dead person can contact us in its fullness, and continue to do."[8]

If there is survival, how important is this to the living? Should the living allow themselves to be influenced by the dead? "It is immensely important to the living, spiritually, philosophically and materially," affirmed Ruby Yeatman. "Reassurance of the continuance of the human personality after death has prevented many a man and woman from committing suicide, has lifted a load of grief from off the shoulders of those who have loved and lost, has replaced despair with hope and given a reason to go on living— and not only to go on living but to live in accordance with spiritual principles, remembering that man is not just a physical being but is body, soul, and spirit and is spirit here and now.

"If by 'should the living allow themselves to be influenced by the dead' you mean should they follow advice regarding this course or that which may be offered by a communicator through a medium, then undoubtedly the wisest course to pursue is to submit such advice to one's own innate intuition and to one's own reasoning power before taking a specific step. Good advice has often been followed by a sitter to his advantage but

7. Beard, *Survival of Death*, pp. 8–9.
8. Ibid., p. 24.

equally false statements have been made and one should bear in mind that those who have died know comparatively little more than those on earth, with some exceptions, and are certainly not infallible. Always bear in mind that the psychic faculties are variable and results can never be guaranteed."

Why do so many believe they have communicated with the dead? Is the belief based on fear of oblivion upon death, or based on true desire to know what lies beyond death? "They believe they have communicated with someone who has died because they have received first-class evidence of the identity of the person, evidence which very often has been unknown to the sitter but is afterwards verified and found to be true. . . . As a general rule, the belief is not based on fear of oblivion after death; the enquiry into the subject arises from the grief experienced by the death of a loved one; in other cases from the sincere desire to know what it may be possible to learn of a life after death, and also to learn more of the whole personality of man and the soul."

So many billions of people have passed over. Where are they all? How can even Infinity accommodate billions of people? "How can even Infinity accommodate the billions of people who have passed over? you ask. How can you envisage Infinity, I ask. How can you possibly know what Infinity can accommodate? Did not St. Paul write: 'In Him we live and move and have our being.' 'Nearer He is than breathing, nearer than hands and feet.' The trouble is that we human beings are limited by Space and Time, or what we designate as space and time, and in reality we know next to nothing of either. Physicists today, I believe, state that Space and Time, as the average person thinks of them, do not exist. We are limited by our earthly condition and by time, as we know it, just as the fish is limited by the ocean. We have to accept that we cannot understand the Creator, the Infinite Mind. How can a finite mind grasp Infinite, Fundamental Reality? The few great contemplative individuals such as Plotinus, St. John of the Cross, St. Teresa of Spain and other saints and contemplative men and women of other beliefs than Christian have experienced something of this wonder and tried to convey to us a little of what it is and what it means.

"The next sphere of activity is not just a place; it is a state. There is no limit to the Infinite, just as there is no beginning and no end. (For me no end is understandable but no beginning is beyond me.) If you accept the theory of Reincarnation, then apparently there would be no lack of 'space' for all the people of earth since Reincarnationists aver that people return again and again to this planet. What about the population explosion?

"Those who have died and are able to communicate tell us that they live not only in another dimension but in another state of being and at a different speed, hence the reason why the generality of people do not see them. Most of the accounts received through mediums, and through automatic writing, tally on the main points and all stress the beauty of the next life and the fact that Time is not as it is here."

Why when reaching the "other side" does one meet loved ones and not strangers from other countries, speaking other languages? "Accounts vary.

Some who have passed over apparently meet their loved ones at once, others appear to be met by someone unknown to them, and again others seem not to know where they are, not realising they are dead. But always there is, although maybe not seen at first, someone waiting to be of help. In Spiritualistic literature, there are various accounts of the states in which certain individuals find themselves. Language apparently presents no difficulty since communication is by means of telepathy. Desire and thought play an important part."

How many past generations can one communicate with? Can one communicate more or perhaps only with departed friends, relatives, and contemporaries, or can one communicate with spirits departed for many generations, such as Plato, Julius Caesar, Erasmus, etc.? "Generally speaking I would say that one would be more likely to receive communication from those who have departed this life within the last hundred years; that is to say as far back as one's own grandfather, or great grandfather. Most people who seek sittings with mediums do so because they want to hear from husband or wife, father or mother, son or daughter or some special friend, and these would fall within the category of contemporaries, more or less.

"There are, however, exceptions. For instance, Patience Worth [who communicated through the American sensitive Mrs. Curran] purported to live 400 years ago. Mrs. Signe Toksvig, the noted Danish writer, who wrote a life of Swedenborg, believed that his influence was manifest in the communications she received through Mrs. Pamela Nash, a well-known trance medium.

"I do not think it is possible to receive communications from such famous people as you have listed above, for I believe that as one progresses in the next world there comes a second death when one passes into another state of being and after that it would be, or is, more difficult to communicate with those on earth. Any communication coming from one passed over so long ago would, I think, be his influence passing down through intermediaries as in the case of *The Scripts of Cleophas* by Miss Geraldine Cummins, the famous automatic writer."

Since most of the major religions believe in life after death, why are these same religions so adamantly opposed to spiritualism and communication with the departed through a medium? "The Churches are opposed to Spiritualism and communication for more than one reason. They may fear the curtailment of their own authority over their congregations; they genuinely think that use of the psychic faculty is, or can be, dangerous. Here they are right in that the wrong use of any faculty can be dangerous; the psychic faculty misused or wrongly used can be a source of trouble, especially to the nervous system of the psychic, but electricity wrongly used can be extremely dangerous, causing death. The Roman Catholic Church, so I gathered from one of its priests, believes that 'to dabble in the occult is dangerous.' Further, this priest said at a debate on the subject that Catholics believed that God had made revelation of himself to mankind in Christ and the Church and that in the teachings of hell, purgatory and heaven they had 'full revelation.' He also believed communication was possible but that it was of the devil. A member of the sect known as the Plymouth Brethren was sure that I should burn in hell for life everlasting. The Archbishop of Canterbury's Committee on Spiritualism accepted its claims and, although the Report was not published at the time, nevertheless the Committee considered that its claims were proved. A large number of clergymen in the Church of England (Protestant faith) accept the truth of Spiritualism and the Churches Fellowship for Psychical and Spiritual Studies has done much to introduce the subject into the churches of all denominations. The Spiritual Frontier in the United States is working along similar lines."

Can you give examples to demonstrate evidence of survival after death? Ruby Yeatman told of a visitation from her father to the clairvoyant and healer, Mrs. Atkinson.

"One morning Mrs. Atkinson said she must speak to me. She said she had, whilst attending to her housework, seen a tall man in a dark blue naval uniform. He had bright blue eyes and dark brown hair. She said to herself, 'The Navy' but he said, 'No, the Army.' She, however, insisted to herself that he was in naval uniform but again he said, 'No, the Army.' However, she persisted in thinking of the Navy when he said sharply, 'NO, THE ARMY.' The reason why Mrs. Atkinson thought the uniform was the Navy and not the Army was because at that time Britain was at war with Germany and the Army wore khaki, but the man, who was my father, chose to show himself in his peacetime uniform of dark blue which, so far as I was concerned, was more evidential since Mrs. Atkinson did not know my father was a regular Army officer. At the same time, in addition to the description, Mrs. Atkinson gave me, as purporting to come from my father, a message of importance to me at the time."

So many people hope to receive communications from famous mediums who have passed on, ones such as Eileen Garrett, but these hopes are not often realized. During the time I knew Eileen, we discussed the possibility of life after death, and I recall one particular instance when I asked her if we would meet again if this was the case. She promised me that if indeed there was a Great Beyond, we would meet there. Apart from that pact, I had no expectation of hearing from Eileen in any fashion. However, a rather unusual event happened while my husband and I were visiting the famous healer Olga Worrall while she was staying in New York. We were in her hotel room, where Olga had just conducted her 9:00 nightly prayer time. Also present were the healer, Lynn Brallier, and Vera Webster, president of Advances In Instruction. Olga glanced up and said, "Eileen Garrett appeared to me, sitting between you, Katy, and your husband. She wanted to tell you that she is very happy that you are writing this book, that she had predicted you would write, and that she was very glad this meeting could take place." I could not help but remember that Eileen had indeed many years ago emphatically told me, "YOU will write!"

In recent correspondence from Don Galloway, well-known sensitive and author of *Inevitable Journey*, he told me of various types of evidential communications, and one in particular dealing with his own father:

"Very quick spontaneous 'flash' communications I have had sometimes from my father who passed over almost eight years ago. In the mean he was a man of few words and even the most exciting or even the most shattering news he ever had to impart would be imparted in a few short phrases.

"In the late summer following his passing, I took mother out for a day's tour of the countryside. I felt strongly my father's presence close to me in the car, and all he had to say was 'Nasser's coming over here—today.' He repeated it and I found this hard to accept. It is noteworthy that he specified 'Today' in view of the fact that the Spirits are often said to have very little sense of our earthly clock-time any more. However, this was in the afternoon. Mother and I arrived home in the evening just in time to switch on the late TV news. First item announced was that President Nasser of Egypt had died suddenly that afternoon."

Don wrote me of another "visit" from his father:

"The following year we had General Elections [British] culminating with the national vote on a Thursday in June. Afternoon of Sunday previous, I had a friend visiting with me and we watched the late afternoon TV news on which it was announced that every possible sign to date favoured Mr. Harold Wilson and the Socialist Party—it was a 'sure thing' they would win the election on Thursday. But, while this was showing, my father seemed to almost burst in on me to announce very clearly 'No—it's Heath—Heath's won—Heath's in—you'll see.' At the time this seemed utterly impossible but, in fact, the following Thursday proved spirit right."

In his role as sensitive, Don Galloway often gives sittings for those deeply grieved by the loss of a loved one. He recalled "a sitting given two years ago to a solicitor's wife, brought to me as a complete stranger. The lady . . . was highly nervous of having a sitting . . . despite the fact she was (so it transpired) desperately grieving over her mother's passing two months before. Additionally, it was shown during the sitting that she and her husband were very devoted and never kept any secrets from each other. However, because she knew he was strongly opposed to the psychic field, etc., this sitting simply HAD to be kept secret. Her general state of distress and anxiety created several barriers to me as a sensitive, but nevertheless I was certainly aware of her discarnate mother's presence and a clear flow of communication from her. Yet although the sitter was taking copious notes in shorthand, she concluded by saying that although she could verify my description of her mother's physical appearance, conditions of passing, and exact personality, the rest of the information she could not understand. She was disappointed and so was I. A week later, the friend who had sent her telephoned me to say this: After a couple of days the young woman (also, like her husband, a lawyer) felt unhappy at having a secret from her husband and so decided to confess to having the sitting. When she read out the notes to him he was amazed, saying 'But all that is almost word for word the last conversation I had with your mother when I visited her in the hospital the night before she died.' "

Olga Worrall, the gifted psychic healer, had been invited to go to Japan to lecture in connection with her healing beliefs but was reluctant to take the long journey. However, she "received" a message from her deceased husband, Ambrose, that he would be with her there and that evidence of this would be given to her. Olga spent six weeks lecturing and healing while in Japan, and she tells how the evidence of Ambrose's promise to be with her there was given:

"He appeared to one of the Japanese professors. . . . The man was so positive that Ambrose was beside me on the platform that he invited *both* of us to his house. He was a man, incidentally, who had never had a psychic experience before in his entire life, and he was most amazed. He described Ambrose perfectly to me—although he had never even seen a picture of Ambrose—and just recently, on a visit to Baltimore, he came to my home and identified a photo of Ambrose as a photo of the man he had seen with me in Japan. Can you imagine anything more evidential? If I had seen Ambrose, it would be open to all the usual charges of imagination, wishful thinking, et cetera, . . . But the fact that Ambrose was visualized by someone else—someone who had never seen Ambrose when Ambrose was alive and someone who saw Ambrose without my even knowing it had happened until he stood up in a church service and told about it afterward —all of this makes it a most significant occurrence. . . .

"He is no kook, no illiterate, no easily persuaded individual. He is what lawyers would call an authoritative or expert witness. His name is Dr. Adachi; he holds a doctorate in political science and is a professor of law at Kwansei Gakuin University in Japan since 1946. . . ."[9]

Andrea Fodor Litkei and I had a lengthy interview in which she related a few of her father's experiences with the world beyond:

"In later years he [Dr. Nandor Fodor] admitted, wistfully, that the glory of his first interview with the Dead had departed, but the unexplainable kernel remained, which led him to the time-worn saw: that it is easier for a camel to pass through the eye of a needle than for a psychic researcher to gain foolproof evidence of survival.

"The second of his personal experiences that could not be lightly brushed aside, began with a sitting in London with Eileen Garrett. Precognition was the principal issue; Captain Hinchcliffe, an ocean-flyer who had perished on an East-to-West transatlantic flight, came through Mrs. Garrett, with information about a similar venture that my father (then political adviser to Lord Rothermere) was keeping his eye on. Lord Rothermere, owner of the leading London newspaper *The Daily Mail*, had offered a $10,000 prize to the first Hungarian airman who would make a non-stop flight from the United States to Budapest, Hungary, in a plane called *Justice For Hungary*. The information given through the medium was that three people were concerned in organizing the flight—one of whom was very worried over the money that had to be raised and second —that the flight might be undertaken within the next three weeks or it would be dangerous. Unknown to anyone *but* my father, *three* people were

9. Cerutti, *Olga Worrall*, pp. 104–5.

involved and *one* of them did have considerable difficulties over the question of funds. Now, this information could have been drawn from his mind, but the second statement could not. He knew *nothing* of an immediate emergency regarding the flight. The next morning, to his astonishment, he received the text of an appeal to the Hungarians of America, in which Captain Endresz, Hungary's ace pilot, and his co-pilot Sandor Magyar concluded with the sentence: 'We must start between June 15th and June 20th.' A striking coincidence with the last day that Captain Hinchcliffe had found favorable.

"As it happened, the actual start was delayed, because of finances, for almost another month, but the flight was successfully completed in July 1931. The slip in time does not dispose of the precognitive element of Captain Hinchcliffe's message/nor does it speak of his survival. However, it happened that a year after the flight, in May, Captain Gyorgy Endresz was delegated to represent Hungary at the First International Congress of Ocean Fliers in Rome. Over the airfield of Rome, before the eyes of the horrified spectators, *Justice For Hungary* took a sudden plunge, hit the earth and exploded. Captain Endresz was burned to death.

"My father had no intentions of trying to establish communications with Captain Endresz, although he was a close and dear friend, but a year later he was having a trance session with Mrs. Agnes Abbot at the London Spiritualist Alliance. She appeared to be in contact with a very excited communicator who 'brought the airplane' and who was quite desperate in trying to get through to him. The messages were good, but they failed to quite convince my father. The next morning, we received a telephone call from Madame Romola Nijinsky, wife of the ballet dancer Nijinsky, and very old friend of ours. Apparently she had had an unplanned sitting with the same medium later that day and was extremely annoyed and mystified that some aviator came through, pestering her, and just would not leave. He kept saying that he crashed to death in Rome, and among other statements, that he flew for a country. This time the evidence—totally unappreciated by the puzzled Madame Nijinsky, but communicated to my father by way of complaining about it—seemed to point to communication from the dead. Subsequent events further confirmed this conclusion.

"A clairvoyant who was present at a lecture given by Dr. Fodor in Brighton came up to him, after he had mentioned the Captain Endresz incident, and said that she could see the aviator standing beside him. My father took little notice of such clairvoyant impressions. *Someone* always sees somebody standing next to the speaker when it comes to psychic matters. But then she said he was holding a small girl in his arms. This struck home. Madame Endresz had given birth to a still-born daughter after the tragedy in Rome. My father asked her if she had any impression of the child's name, since he knew he could check up on it. Then came the thunderbolt . . . Andre . . . An . . . Andrea!"

Andrea continued: "That's me . . . Captain Endresz had picked me up in his arms many times and had also placed me in an airplane where we had our picture taken together, and inscribed the photograph 'Justice For Andrea Fodor.' The clairvoyant had not said baby or infant; she had said small girl. Could this clairvoyant vision, then, have been the final message from a very persistent man? . . ."

Andrea went on to tell how, sadly, Mrs. Abbot's mediumship deteriorated and she was later accused of fraud. "Many sitters demand too much of the medium and almost push them into the easy path of deception," said Andrea. "This is one of the reasons why Dr. Fodor believed that mediumistic and related phenomena should be approached on psychological and not legal ground. . . . The history of psychic research has proven that not all is fraud, nor all is genuine. Which, as my father said, amounts to this: it must be a heart-breaking job for a dead man to try to prove that he is alive."

And does Andrea believe in life after death? For her, as for most others knowledgeable in the subject, it is not a simple answer.

"Emotionally, I believe in life after death because it probably suits my unconscious purposes. And, emotionally one wants to believe because one doesn't want to think this is the end. . . . Intellectually, I have trouble believing because the factors involved stun the human mind with actually what our capabilities are. And, if it is true, then we are using such a limited amount of our capabilities that it is really a shameful sin that if we have that capability within us that we live our lives the way we do. However, looking at it from an intellectual level, because the physicists have probed some of the secrets of the universe, it does seem to support the theory of some kind of survival. The main question is, does the personality survive along with the human being or not? The scientists have looked into the macrocosm and found no end. They have looked into the microcosm and found no end. We are born and we started from somewhere and changed our form. Therefore I would have to postulate we are going somewhere and we will change our form. So, if we forget about the personality, it is very hard not to believe in survival. If you think of the human personality with all its silly little memories and a lot of the neuroses that go to make up the memories, then it's intellectually a little staggering to really say that 'Yes, there is life after death.' Emotionally, I definitely believe in it and, of course, there are too many instances, not one at a time taken separately, but if you take the conglomerate of so many legends and instances through the ages, the sheer weight of happenstances that have occurred should make us at least take a good look, and a good chance for intellectually believing as well."

It seems incredible to me that in the shortness of one life span I was blessed with the extraordinary good fortune of meeting such individuals of stature as Eileen Garrett, Dr. Nandor Fodor, Professor Edward McNall Burns, Lawrence LeShan, Alex Tanous, Dr. John Conley, Dr. Robin Rankow, Ruby Yeatman, Paul Beard, Jozsef Gyimesi, Professor W. Tenhaeff and countless others. And, surely, someone up there must have been looking over my shoulder the day I met Olga Worrall.

How to describe Olga Worrall? She has been called by her biographer, Edwina Cerutti, the "mystic with the healing hands." Her gift of spiritual healing, for which she is world-renowned, was explored in the chapters of this book on psychic healing. A warm, sincere, extemely caring individual, Olga, drawing from her own psychic experiences, answers some perplexing questions on survival after life.

What is dying like? "Death," said Olga, "is actually as painless as sleep. Disease may bring pain but death eliminates it. Death is no more to be feared than sleep, which most of us welcome. Did you ever read the statement on dying made by Sir William Osler, the famous physician? . .

"He said," Olga repeated from memory, "that 'most human beings not only die like heroes, but in my wide clinical experience, die really without pain or fear. There is as much oblivion about the last hours as about the first, and therefore, men fill their minds with specters that have no reality.' "[10]

"According to Olga," Edwina Cerutti writes, "dying is really birth into the spirit world. It occurs when the body of flesh is no longer useful to the spirit. The spirit leaves the body in exactly the same way as when the body passes into the sleep state each night."

As to the physical sensations at the moment of death, Olga says: "A lightness and feeling of peace is felt as the spirit slowly leaves the body. Then there is a sensation of floating as the spirit adjusts itself and stands apart from the body, which can be seen by the departing spirit. The room and all persons present are visible and the departing spirit will hear their comments. Should there be weeping the spirit will try to assure the mourners that he is well and alive, but in most cases they will not hear him because they have not developed the gift of clairaudience.

"Gradually the scene takes on a misty experience as the spirit slowly retunes its consciousness from the world of the flesh to the world of the spirit. This may take the better part of an hour, after which the departing soul becomes slowly conscious of the new realm in which it will live, and the earth no longer seems real.

"There is always someone waiting to greet a new soul entering the world of spirits. It may be a loved one, a close friend, or simply someone who has been appointed to show him the way. Those who do not believe in life after death are quite confused when they find themselves in conscious existence after death. Many of them refuse to believe that they are among the so-called dead because the spirit world is so real to them in their new state of consciousness. It is only after meeting many other departed souls whom they knew to be dead that they begin to realize they are indeed in the new dimension."[11]

Why do most people not consider the possibility of life after death until they have experienced a loss? Olga feels the blame rests with "the traditional heaven and hell business on which so many of us are raised. . . . That gets to be unpalatable after a while—sort of too pat a solution, too clearcut—so we just shove the whole survival bit into some dark corner of our minds and rarely think about any of it until we come face to face with

10. Ibid., pp. 70–71.
11. Ibid., pp. 71–72.

death ourselves, or else lose somebody close to us."[12] She stresses that "no matter what the cause of death may be—no matter what!—the spirit lives on. No soul is ever lost."[13]

How can a sensitive use his or her knowledge and understanding of the spirit world to help the living deal with death? Olga, for one, believes that "the burning question for all mankind has always been: If a man dies, shall he live again?" Consequently, she feels it is important to use her psychic gifts to prove human survival beyond the grave, not only because she believes this knowledge would encourage and comfort the bereaved, but also because it would offer meaning and purpose to all who live. Part of her mission is to teach what to expect in the afterworld so that preparation and adjustment may be accomplished before the transition occurs. Another aspect of Olga's life mission is to provide proof to those in need of understanding and acceptance of survival of death.

When asked how her psychic gift helped in this respect, Olga replied:

"When I transmit a highly evidential message from a spirit to a loved one he has left behind, that's proof. Even the most skeptical have to stop and think: 'Where did she get this information that only Cousin Harry or Aunt Mary knew; and how could she get it from him or her unless, in some form, in some way, Cousin Harry or Aunt Mary had told her; and how could they have told her if they were not alive? . . .' "[14]

Of her own loss and confrontation with death Olga said, "Ambrose [her husband] and I knew that life continued after death. If we could better understand that we are here for a brief spell, that we begin our existence here and then in 50, 60, 70, 80, maybe a hundred years, we are ready then to go into the higher life, which is an octave higher. You have a piano with your octaves, and you go from one octave to the other. Yet, it is one piano. So, it means that it is one universe, but in different octaves. And so we go into the next dimension and we leave the physical things behind because it's a physical world and when we go into the next dimension, we will be functioning in a more refined world. . . . I want to tell those who have suffered a bereavement to understand that God does not create to destroy, and those who we love we will continue to be with when we join each other."

While I was visiting with Olga in her home in Baltimore, she told me the following story, wherein she saw the wife of Aldous Huxley appear shortly after her death: "The first time I ever met Aldous Huxley, I knew nothing about the Huxleys. Aldous Huxley was at Wainright House and he was to give a lecture. In the morning, the group of speakers were at the table. My husband was one of them. We were sitting there listening to the men, as each speaker told what they were going to talk about. I became clairvoyant and I saw a woman standing next to Aldous Huxley. She said, 'I am Maria. I am his wife. I just passed away recently and you tell Aldous that the poetry he read to me, I heard every word, and there were times when

12. Ibid., p. 69.
13. Ibid., pp. 86, 87.
14. Ibid., pp. 62–63.

he thought he was wasting his time and that perhaps I wasn't even there. You tell him he didn't waste his time. I heard it.' And then she proceeded to give some very personal messages and Aldous Huxley bowed his head and wept. The group at the table were told by him that his wife had passed away two months before, and he confirmed that he had indeed wondered if she had heard what he was reading to her or whether he was wasting his time. It was a comfort to him to know she was aware of his presence."

It really is not important whether the author of this book goes along with any of the philosophies expounded. In all honesty, I am still exploring many areas. What *is* important is that the views of knowledgeable individuals, and those highly respected in their field, be expressed. Then you can judge for yourself. If you *are* satisfied with the answers, then you may wish to explore more. If you *are not* content with the statements, then you may also wish to explore further.

I would like to close with this thought from Coleridge:

> What if you slept?
> And what if, in your sleep, you dreamed?
> And what if, in your dream, you went to heaven
>   and there plucked a strange and beautiful flower?
> And what if, when you awoke, you had the flower
>   in your hand?
> Ah, what then?

18

Automatic Writing / Psychic Dreams

A great deal of controversy exists over automatic writing, particularly regarding its source and the uses to which it should be put. There are those who claim automatic writing comes from the subconscious or super-consciousness of the person who is attempting it. Others believe it comes from a discarnate spirit, and is therefore strong evidence of survival after death. Still others maintain that it is being received telepathically by the writer from another living person.

The late Eileen Garrett, medium, psychic researcher, and spiritualist, held to the theory that automatic writing originated from within the writer himself:

"I have used it in different phases and periods of my own work. I am sure that it is an expression of the self, and that it can be used as a means both to reach the subconscious *and* to reach the highest levels of the superconsciousness. It is used successfully by many people as a means of producing communication telepathically, and I believe that as such it can be used most constructively."[1]

However, Eileen cautions against the use of automatic writing in other instances:

"There is only one place where I am a little hesitant to advise its use, and that is as a means and ways to bridge the gulf between life and after-life. I have seen examples of automatic writing that I was sure were no more than the submerged wish fulfillment process of the subconscious mind, in which the dream becomes a dangerous manifestation of wishful thinking, and reality for the time being becomes effaced."[2]

How is automatic writing accomplished? What does one have to do? Ruby Yeatman, with the College of Psychic Studies in London for almost thirty-five years, offers these instructions:

"Sit quietly and comfortably at a table with a large sheet of paper before

---

1. Garrett, *Telepathy*, p. 158.
2. Ibid., p. 158.

you; hold a pencil lightly in your hand on the paper; let the conscious mind be quiescent. Sit at the same time and on the same day once or twice (not more) a week.

"Remember that once the door is open, it is open to good, bad and indifferent and, before any sitting, I would myself repeat the Lord's Prayer and I would ask for protection and that unpleasant influences might be kept away; even so interference does sometimes happen and then it is essential to close down, that is, stop writing. Always bear in mind that *you*, the incarnate person, must be in command of the situation.

"Once the conscious mind is quiescent, there can be an upwelling of the unconscious mind and some really remarkably fine matter can be forthcoming, but it is *not* communication from the Unseen."

Ruby advises questioning the "communicator" to establish his or her "credentials" and the validity of the message.

"It is necessary to establish, if possible, the identity of your communicator and to be satisfied on this point before accepting as 'gospel truth' statements which may be made. Some very fine communication has been received through this form of psychic development but it does seem to be open to considerable interference. Here, however, as with all psychic work, true and good motive, a sincere desire to be of service, combined with trustworthy and intelligent cooperators in the Unseen, will give good results as the power is co-ordinated.

"It may take weeks before anything at all is written and scribbles only may come for some time."

For those of you who may have attempted automatic writing and have met with little success, Theon Wright, an investigator in this field, describes the enormous amount of patience required in order to achieve it:

"At first I used only what is known as 'hand control.' This is a technique in which the medium [the person attempting automatic writing] merely relaxes and permits his hand to move freely across the paper, holding a pencil. The words at first are usually scrawled in large characters and it requires concentration on the part of the writer to avoid directing his own hand. It is obvious that a mixture of concentration and relaxation at the same time is not easy to attain. For months I continued this regularly, always alone, in an effort to develop this skill. At first the messages I received were short, and not particularly illuminating. . . . As I continued, the script became smaller, the wording more concise and I found less difficulty adjusting my own reactions to the control that seemed to be exercised."[3]

Is automatic writing to be done alone or can others besides the writer participate? You can indeed sit with another person, whether it be your spouse, a friend, or a relative. Affirms Ruby Yeatman, "It would be, probably, good for you to sit together; in fact, I would advise it." There are groups of automatic writers who practice what is known as cross-correspondence. This type of automatic writing consists of related frag-

3. Wright, *The Open Door*, pp. 331–32.

ments of messages coming from various automatic writers, and produced time and time again over long intervals.

Dr. Gardner Murphy, well-known psychologist, author, and former president of the Society for Psychical Research in London and the American Society for Psychical Research in New York, told the following story:

"A skeptical friend of mine had been reading the cross correspondence material because I had told him that as a civilized person with scientific pretensions he ought to know something about psychical research. He was drowsy that afternoon; he put a pencil between his thumb and finger and dozed off. Then the telephone rang and he was annoyed at being interrupted in his nap. As he answered the phone he looked down at the pad, and on the sheet was written 'I hear the bell.' He wasn't sure he was going to have anything to do with automatic writing, but in the very midst of this self-induced state it was starting! And very often automatic writing, in one form or another, starts and goes on as far as it is allowed to go."

Although an advocate of automatic writing, Dr. Murphy nonetheless urges caution: "Now, I hasten to agree that it can easily go too far. It can lead a somewhat vulnerable person into developing a form of dissociation which he cannot control. There is some risk. But this is true of a great many things. It is true of drug research . . . but we don't stop all research because of the dangers involved."[4]

Of what importance is automatic writing? Dr. Murphy replies:

"Now, it must be stressed that the production of an automatic phenomenon is not in itself important. It is merely a vehicle by means of which the paranormal may or may not be expressed. An automatic script, for example, is no more significant than it would be if I were to tell you that there is a boat drifting by itself near the coast. How good a boat, how useful a boat, how difficult it will be to rescue the crew—we don't know. The question is not whether you can produce an automatism—the chances are that many of you can. The question is whether the automatist becomes a *useful* vehicle for veridical messages. There is a great deal of story-telling in the sphere of automatism. But the material might contain . . . messages having to do with a clear-cut telepathic line of communication with a distant individual, or even having to do with seeming communication between the living and the deceased."[5]

Can automatic writing occur in any other forms? It appears that automatic writing can be achieved in the waking or dreaming stage. Many times it arrives in the form of psychic dreams, as attested to by many literary greats.

William Blake claimed that a good portion of his poetry had been "dictated," and when finishing his illustrations for Milton's *Paradise Lost*, he wrote in a letter: "I may praise it, since I dare not pretend to be any other than the Secretary; the Authors are in Eternity."

4. Gardner Murphy, "The Discovery of Gifted Sensitives," *Journal of the American Society for Psychical Research* 63 (1969), no. 1.
5. Ibid.

The famous French writer and founder of the surrealist movement in the 1920s, André Breton, used automatic writing to produce several of his books, *Les Champs Magnetiques* and *Poisson Soluble*. Anna Balakian, Breton's biographer, discusses his philosophy of automatic writing and its connection with dreams.

"André Breton thought of automatic writing as 'magic dictation' in the general category of dreams, as a verbal continuation of these, the overflowing of the fountain whose source is the collective self, the universal conscience. Breton felt that automatic writing had the power of hallucination over its practitioner, as evidenced by the state of euphoria in which he . . . found [himself] at the end of each day of writing."[6]

Breton found the experience so rewarding, he conditioned his body to be even more receptive:

"André Breton was eating less and less; and as he confesses candidly, the days of total fasting weakened his physical stability and produced a psychic state more conducive to automatic writing and spontaneous dreaming."[7]

Apparently many of Robert Louis Stevenson's stories were derived from his dreams with the help of some discarnate spirits he referred to as the "little people." In her book *Remembered on Waking*, Vera S. Staff relates his "habit of 'setting himself to sleep with tales' and then began to write them down. He said he was able to do this through the help of 'the little people who manage man's internal theatre' and he declared that these Brownies (as he called them) became disciplined like the author, to write for business purposes. . . . When a story had come to him in sleep he says there was 'At last a jubilant leap to wakefulness, with the cry of 'I have it, that'll do! . . .' He goes on: 'That which is done when I am up and about is by no means necessarily mine, since all goes to show the Brownies have a hand in it even then. . . . I am sometimes tempted to suppose that the man is no story teller at all . . . so that the whole of my published fiction should be the single-handed product of some Brownie, some Familiar, some *unseen collaborator.*' "

In *Breakthrough to Creativity*, Dr. Shafika Karagulla tells of an odd dream Niels Bohr, the famous atomic scientist, had when he was a student. He dreamed he was on a sun made up of burning gas, and planets appeared moving about the sun, connected by minute threads. Upon waking, he had the atom model.

A cautionary note: "The student of psychic dreams should be a sensible person if he is not to get lost in a world of fantasy, and for this reason he might well decide to join a group of investigators with a leader who would be able to offer some guidance in interpretation. Suitable groups are not easily formed or found, but one of the societies for psychic study could be asked to help. . . . And the group most likely to foster a gift for visionary dreaming is one formed for the practice of meditation. But the dreams must be allowed to happen naturally. . . . Few visions of spirituality are

6. Balakian, *André Breton*, pp. 61–62.
7. Ibid., p. 46.

given in a lifetime to one person, but a single revelation on the road to Damascus is enough. . . .

"Where such a group meditates for specific purposes their work might be greatly helped by what their dreams reveal, for the inexpressible can be better appreciated by a symbol which stirs the imagination. Whether the symbol arises from the deep unconscious or is shown through the agency of a discarnate being is immaterial."[8]

An extremely intriguing philosophical view is put forth here: "The weight of evidence that other intelligences besides our own are actively engaged with our dreaming selves is bound to grow. . . .

"The development of psychic dreaming should be considered alongside the development of other psychic faculties, as part of the unfoldment of the whole man and woman, the realization of their potential. The most deeply impressive dreams, those with the greatest significance, have been found to be the psychic ones—those which are concerned with the soul.

"The message of the Soul to the soul has a quality of joy and beauty, of understanding penetration, which we associate with the divine. And it has another quality of equal importance—the psychic dream is not an *isolate* experience: it is *given*, whatever its source. It is a communication from One to another and therefore demonstrates a togetherness, a proof that we are not alone, even in the hours of sleep. . . .

"Creative artists know the power of the imagination to bring to life in their minds books, pictures, symphonies: even so, psychic dreams whether arising from images of waking life, or those never seen on earth, can enrich our lives, revitalize us, and reveal truth to us so that we may face the nightmares of the material world with new courage and confidence."[9]

The Ouija board is another form of automatic writing. A board with various designs on it, including letters of the alphabet, it also has an accompanying planchette. Hands are placed lightly on the movable planchette, and the "energy" from the hands moves the object toward various symbols in the hope of ultimately spelling out a message. The Ouija board is often used as a parlor game as a way to seek telepathic communication or unconscious thoughts, and other times as a way to seek messages from the "other side."

J. Gaither Pratt, in *The Psychic Realm: What Can You Believe?*, states that the Ouija board "can be interesting and quite good fun." However, Dr. Pratt does warn players that if the supposed "communicator" should become unpleasant or make threats, then it might be wise to either abandon use of the board or establish a rule that only friendly communications will be acceptable if continuing. In the event the players believe ESP results occur and continue for a time, Dr. Pratt advises that someone knowledgeable of psi phenomena should be contacted to evaluate the results.

The history of the Ouija board—also known as planchette or ESP Board—is quite ancient. It was used by the Greeks and Romans for receiving messages from the spirits in the "unseen world." During the Middle Ages,

8. Staff, *Remembered on Waking*, pp. 145, 146.
9. Ibid., pp. 147, 148.

it was considered an instrument of the Devil by Church authorities. And during the reign of Charles II of England, the use of the planchette as part of fortunetelling was considered treason against the king and punishable by death.

Hans Holzer describes the type of "communication" often received on the board and advises caution in its use:

"Frequently, communications obtained through an Ouija board are meaningless even down to the words and sentences, which do not seem to jell into any intelligible pattern. I suspect that the poltergeist-like unconscious of a sitter may thus express itself, or perhaps a genuine nonphysical communicator, in the same condition, has somehow gotten hold of a communication line but cannot make himself clear. . . .

"Those who wish to use the Ouija board as a parlor game I advise to think twice. There is always the possibility—rare, I admit, but conceivable —that one of those playing the board is a genuine trance medium without realizing it.

"In such a case, the board can become an easy entrance for a discarnate person who might next take over the personality of the medium and manifest under conditions where no controls are possible."[10]

Andrea Fodor Litkei presents a more modern interpretation of the Ouija board:

"Today we have a more modern interpretation as to how the ESP board works. The most popular theory is that the answers to the questions come from your unconscious mind and that autonomous muscular impulses, according to Jung, 'unconscious motor phenomena' . . . are responsible for its movement.

"In plain language, you are pushing it yourself, without cheating or knowing that you are pushing it, by imperceptible, nervous, muscular movements of your own hands with your unconscious supplying you with the answers."[11]

It would appear, however, that in certain instances the Ouija board can produce telepathic or precognitive messages. Andrea relates the following interesting story:

"A mother and daughter were playing with the ESP board. The mother was an ardent believer in this sort of thing, whereas the daughter scoffed at it as nonsense and only played with her mother to please her. One afternoon the daughter decided that she would prove to her mother how nonsensical she was in sticking to her beliefs and purposely pushed the pointer until she spelt out the message that her mother was to go at once to Selfridge's (the largest department store in London) because at 3:30 she would meet a friend there whom she had not seen for twenty years. At which, the mother grabbed her hat and coat and started out of the house saying that she had only five minutes to make it. The daughter pleaded with her not to go, admitting that she had made the whole thing up to prove to her that these things did not exist. The mother said that neverthe-

10. Holzer, *ESP and You*, p. 73.
11. Litkei, *ESP*, pp. 76–77.

less she believed in it and that she was going to Selfridge's anyway. Imagine the daughter's horrified surprise when the mother came home a little while later with the friend of her prediction and that they had met at exactly 3:30!"[12]

How long can automatic writing continue and how much material can be produced?

Pearl Curran, a St. Louis housewife, began using the Ouija board when she was thirty years old and the pointer spelled out these words, recorded by Pearl's mother: "Many moons ago I lived. Again I come—Patience Worth is my name."

According to J. Gaither Pratt and Naomi Hintze, authors of *The Psychic Realm: What Can You Believe?*, "Patience wrote over 5000 poems and in the 1918 *Anthology of Magazine Verse* and *Yearbook of American Poetry* her poems received higher ratings than those of Edna St. Vincent Millay, Amy Lowell and Edgar Lee Masters. Nearly 4 million words were written during the almost quarter of a century that Patience Worth was communicating. Henry Holt, a discriminating publisher, much interested in psychic phenomena, published three of her books, saying that he considered it literature of a high order. He took the view that the writing may have originated in the 'cosmic soul' speculating that there might be inflow from 'strings of postcarnate personalities—if there are such.' In his book *The Case of Patience Worth*, Walter F. Pierce (former president of the Society for Psychical Research in London) indicated that Patience was most likely what she claimed—the "spirit of a girl who had lived in the 17th century."[13]

Is there any way to ascertain that the messages received through automatic writing are indeed from the "other side?" Theon Wright, a present-day investigator of automatic writing, believes we can't be sure:

"Automatic writing . . . is a physical act. Someone writes." Yet, "the way in which automatic communication [writing] takes place indicates in general that it is a transmission of thought between entities in an area of existence that is not physical and yet is capable of transmission of no physical thought into the physical realm of the human brain. Since it takes the form of conscious transmission of thought, or reaction to thought, when it reaches this physical plane, it is difficult to know with finite certainty what is being received."[14]

So, the controversy over the source of automatic writing continues. In addition to the possibility of receiving messages from a discarnate spirit or from the automatist's unconscious via the board, there is also the possibility of messages being received telepathically from another living person or through precognition. In any event, the musicians, poets, writers, artists, and scientists who have utilized automatic writing seem to consider it a precious gift of communication—regardless of the source.

12. Ibid., pp. 77–78.
13. Pratt and Hintze, *The Psychic Realm: What Can You Believe?*, p. 182.
14. Wright, *The Open Door*, p. 325.

CHAPTER

19

Reincarnation

What is meant by reincarnation? Reincarnation comes from Latin and can be translated as "becoming flesh again." It is defined as the taking of a new body by the soul after the death of its previous body. This passing of the soul from one body to another is called *transmigration*, which simply means a crossing from one place to another. Beliefs differ as to the exact time interval between death and reincarnation of the soul. Some people contend the soul enters the new body upon the death of the old one. Others believe the soul must wait a long time before assuming a new body. Although some believers hold to the opinion that the soul may reincarnate into either a higher or lower form of life, most believers claim the soul is always returned to the same species.

How do different cultures view the idea of reincarnation? The idea of reincarnation, or the passage of one soul from a former body to another one, has been held since early times. Many primitive people have a belief in the transmigration of souls. The Australian aborigines claim that an infant is the reincarnation of a dead ancestor. Tribes in Indonesia believe the soul is continually reborn, but that it must wait its turn in sacred animals before reincarnating.

The Irish Celts held strong views on reincarnation, probably stemming from their contact with the Druids in France and Britain. Similar to the Druids, they believed that after death the soul left its body and occupied another. However, the second body could be a ghostly apparition instead of a living organism. Further, the Irish Celts claimed the transmigration from one body to another was accomplished only by heroes who died in battle.

Many famous Greek philosophers and writers, including Pythagoras, Plato, Plotinus, and Empedocles, believed in the transmigration of souls. The Greeks claimed that the soul could occupy many bodily shapes, not just human ones. They felt the future destiny of a person depended upon which body his soul had occupied in previous reincarnations. It is possible these beliefs were derived from Egyptian sources. However, many scholars now claim the Greek ideas on reincarnation were due to contact with India.

Reincarnation is the principal doctrine of several religions initially established in India. In Hinduism, the soul begins a new existence after the death of the body. Its past moral conduct determines the condition of the soul and the time of its rebirth. This is called karma, or the total sum of life. Reincarnation of the soul takes place eternally unless, through great devotion and arduous effort, it can free itself. Such release from the eternal cycle is considered possible for only a select and very religious few. The Buddhists do not accept the soul as such. Their doctrine claims the soul is an illusion. Therefore, reincarnation is but an idea of man and not of the universe. While it is true that human existences are produced and reproduced according to karma, or past actions, this does not signify rebirth. The Buddhist believes the individual is not a separate body but, rather, a part of a universal oneness. Man keeps returning to this world because of desire. Only when all desire ceases, and the individual becomes a saint, will the body be able to attain this oneness.

What views are held for and against reincarnation? Dr. Raynor C. Johnson makes a strong case for acceptance of reincarnation:

"If the case for pre-existence [survival of death] is considered a strong one, then the idea of re-incarnation presents no logical difficulties, whatever be the emotional reaction to it. What the soul has done once by the process of incarnation in a physical body, it can presumably do again. . . . We should of course bear in mind that what is meant by the phrase 'have lived before' is not that the physical form of Raynor Johnson has lived on earth previously, but rather that Raynor Johnson is only a particular and temporary expression of an underlying immortal soul which has adopted previous and quite possibly different appearances. . . . We may reflect on the pageant of living things, the power which builds an oak tree from an acorn, or a human child from a fertilized ovum."[1]

At present, the facts of physical evolution are generally accepted. These state that all living creatures have evolved *physically* from each other over a period of several hundred million years. Nature keeps experimenting with different types reborn from older, outdated species. All creatures began in the sea and some eventually crawled out of the water onto the land. Soon adaptation made land creatures fly as birds in the sky. Eventually, physical evolution brought about the era of the dinosaurs—and also their destruction when these enormous creatures could not adapt to change.

Near-man appeared on the scene some one million years ago and he has been undergoing physical evolution ever since. First as Peking man, then Neanderthal man, then Cro-Magnon man, and finally as modern man.

If the physical body can go through so many evolutionary changes, is it unreasonable to think that the soul can also go through evolution? Cannot the soul evolve and change by going through one reincarnation after the other? These are penetrating questions that every person interested in

1. Johnson, *The Imprisoned Splendour*, pp. 381–82.

reincarnation may care to explore. The very fact that the soul is born into a body leads one to ask: Can the soul be reborn again and again? It would appear that the soul, as well as the body, has much to gain through evolutionary rebirth, change, and adjustment to a new environment.

According to Ruby Yeatman, "The theory of reincarnation is accepted, or seems to be, by many spirits in the next world and is equally rejected by others. . . . The scales seem to be equally balanced."

Olga Worrall makes the observation that many people who accept the idea of reincarnation are not particularly happy in their present existence and would welcome the idea of past lives. Olga advises that in "messages" received from her deceased husband, Ambrose, he says, "We do not reincarnate." Olga also stated that in a "communication" from Eileen Garrett that Eileen had advised similarly "we do not reincarnate."

Is it possible that, just as there are different types of blood required for transfusions, some reincarnations can conceivably take place "instantly" because the specific force or energy is the "type" required? And is it equally conceivable that Ambrose and Eileen may have a type of energy that may have already fully evolved to a higher state where no reincarnations are necessary? Perhaps this may account for the varying reports from those on the "other side" regarding reincarnation. Another theory propounded by some psychics such as Dr. Robert Leichtman, is that those who communicate from the other side may not have been there long enough to know whether we reincarnate or not.

Can people return in the animal state? Although there are those who maintain that the soul may reincarnate into a higher or lower form of life, most believers claim the soul is always returned to the same species.

"The Hindus," states Ruby Yeatman, "believe that people do return in an animal state—this is the theory of transmigration which is held by many in the East and is a belief which originated in the East."

Professor W. C. Tenhaeff, Director of the Parapsychological Institute in Utrecht, Holland, while accepting the possibility of reincarnation, scoffs at the idea of man returning in animal form such as a cat or dog as "nonsense."

Why is it some people believe they have lived before? "Many people accept this belief because they say they can remember their past lives, or at least one of them," explains Ruby Yeatman. "Witness Joan Grant and the many books she has written based upon what she believes to be her previous lives. Others accept the belief because people such as Dr. Ian Stevenson of Wills Eye Hospital, Virginia, and Dr. Leslie Weatherhead of the City Temple London, also many others, have written setting forth cases which they consider offer reasonable evidence for the reality and truth of reincarnation. Theosophists accept this belief as a truth.

"It is true many people do claim to have been someone of importance in a previous life. This it seems is due to vanity on their part and a desire to make up for being a nobody in this life—an inferiority complex, as it were: 'When I was a king in Babylon, you were a Christian slave!' Yes, it would definitely seem that the ego is involved."

Is there any proof of reincarnation? Ruby Yeatman states: "There is no proof of reincarnation, any more than there is of human survival; by proof, in this context, is meant scientific proof. The believers in reincarnation believe that the evidence offered by such investigators as those previously mentioned, and by the claims of the Theosophical Society and like societies does and do offer proof of the plurality of lives. The theory of reincarnation is accepted, or seems to be, by many spirits in the next world and is equally rejected by many others. . . . The scales seem to be equally balanced."

An opposing view is maintained by Dr. Arthur W. Osborn, who finds reincarnation acceptable based on his own observations of ESP:

"The following propositions seem reasonable:

"1. On general principles, reincarnation may be expected to occur.

"2. Psi phenomena [ESP] imply that consciousness can function beyond normal physical limits. Survival after death therefore is both conceivable and probable especially in the light of 'out of body' experiences.

"3. Some memories may be genuine recollections of past lives and careful research is making good progress towards proof or at least making reincarnation the most probable hypothesis.

"4. Reincarnation, even if true, has not necessarily any spiritual value as long as it confines attention to a temporal sequence."[2]

What research, if any, is being done in the field of reincarnation? As both Miss Yeatman and Dr. Osborn have stated, much scientific research is being conducted that tends to support the theory of reincarnation. One of the leading scientists in this study is Dr. Ian Stevenson of the University of Virginia School of Medicine. It is Dr. Stevenson's task to investigate cases of alleged "rebirth," especially when they involve children who claim to have lived previous lives. In a number of such cases, Dr. Stevenson has verified that the children he examined remembered detailed information about a dead person, including minute details of his or her everyday life.

While it is true that remembrance of things past could be a form of ESP, such as retrocognition, Dr. Stevenson revealed that several of his young subjects were born with birthmarks corresponding exactly with the marks on "their" previous bodies. Some of these birthmarks were so unusual that the doctor had to conclude they were a strong case in support of rein-carnation—and not merely coincidence.

I have mentioned Dr. Ian Stevenson and his work because he is a pioneer in the area of reincarnation investigation. However, many other scientists and parapsychologists in the United States, England, and India are also working in this field, such as Dr. Authur Guirdham (author of *The Cathars and Reincarnation*), Frank Smythe (in *Man, Myth and Magic #8*), and Frank Edwards (*Stranger Than Science*).

Does believing in reincarnation tend to encourage its occurrence? Andrea Fodor Litkei presents an intriguing theory as to whether belief might foster psychic phenomena:

"Is there anything to the mechanism of belief that somehow enables

2. Osborn, *The Meaning of Personal Existence*, p. 211.

things to happen that would not happen under circumstances of disbelief and outright cynicism? On the one hand we would be inclined to think that belief helps, since it is a well-known fact that mediums can be put off by the suspicious attitude of an accusing researcher and operate far better in the presence of a sympathetic one. Yet things do happen in the face of the most blatant skepticism. Can we come to the conclusion that in spite of surface skepticism there is an underlying emotional belief although there may be an intellectual denial?

"To support the theory that there may be some unknown quantity set in motion through the act of believing (and I am not implying faith—rather a conviction, a knowing), the Eastern countries that accept these phenomena at face value certainly seem to have a preponderance of them. Barring superstition and primitive folklore, the authenticated and well-documented cases are far more abundant than in the countries of the West.

"Reincarnation is rampant in India, whereas there are only rare, isolated instances attested to it in the West. India believes in reincarnation, ergo, it has its examples to prove it. England has more hauntings than most countries, etc.

"The Tibetan mind is necessary to produce the phenomenon of . . . a book such as the *Tibetan Book of the Dead*, which contains instructions to the dead on how to prevent the return of the spirit to earth and stop its connections, so as not to hinder its progress elsewhere."[3]

At this point, I would like to cite two cases as possible examples of reincarnation. The first occurred in India and involved a young girl named Shanti Devi. Her experience is described by Colin Wilson:

"She [Shanti Devi] was born in Delhi in 1926. When she was seven, she informed her parents that she had been born before, in a town called Muttra. She described her life in some detail—how she had been married and had three children—she died when giving birth to the third. Her name, she said, had been Ludgi. Her parents assumed this was pure imagination. But in 1935, a man called at the house on business, and Shanti Devi started with amazement, declaring that he was her husband's cousin. The man confirmed that he was from Muttra, and that he had a cousin who had lost his wife, named Ludgi, in childbirth ten years earlier. Ludgi's husband was brought to the house—without telling the girl he was expected; she recognised him instantly and threw herself into his arms. Taken to Muttra, she was able to point out various people and places correctly, and converse with relatives of the dead Ludgi in local dialect, although Shanti Devi had been taught in Hindustani."[4]

A commission was set up to investigate the background of Shanti Devi. It found that she recognized many landmarks—even though Shanti had never visited Muttra before. Further, she recognized her two eldest children by name, but not the child whose birth had caused her death. Although several scientists raised the question of telepathy, this was discounted by a majority of the commission. The final report asserted the case of Shanti Devi to be one of probable reincarnation.

The second case took place in the United States and England. It is cited

3. Litkei, *ESP*, pp. 126–28.
4. Colin Wilson, *The Occult: A History*, pp. 514–15.

as an example of either reincarnation or *déjà vu* or both. *Déjà vu* is translated from the French as "already seen." It can best be defined as seeing some thing or some place for the first time, and yet feeling that you have somehow seen it before. This is what happened to Barry Bingham, president and editor of the *Louisville Courier-Journal and Times*:

"Several times in my life, I have had a curious and arresting experience. I have felt that everything I was seeing and hearing had been seen and heard before, and that I knew exactly what was going to happen next.

"My own most memorable experience with déjà vu occurred a good many years ago. . . . I had had at that time a recurrent dream over a period of several months. In it, I found myself approaching a very tall and beautiful building that stood in an open space of green grass. The scene was always bathed in the serene light of a morning that follows a rainy night. . . .

"I knew, in the way we know some things in dreams, that the earth had just undergone some vast cataclysm, and that the band of people I was about to join were the sole survivors of the human race come together to make a plan for the future. The men and women I saw as I neared them were not familiar to me. They were not sad, nor ill, nor distraught, but wrapt in a kind of mute ecstasy as they moved toward the majestic doors of the edifice."[5]

Bearing in mind Mr. Bingham's dream, let's listen to his description of his first trip to Salisbury, England, many years later:

"One day I found myself in front of Salisbury Cathedral in England for the first time in my life. Suddenly I stood stock still, hardly daring to breathe. This ancient church, waiting for me so quietly in its setting of dewy greensward, was the building of my dream in every detail. I knew the soaring line of the spires, the intricate carving of the doorway, the very feel of the stones under my feet. It was as though I had spent year upon year of my life in that very spot.

"Stumbling into the church, still dazed, and awed by my experience, I moved up the aisle and sat down for a moment to rest. . . . As I raised my eyes, I saw directly before me the cenotaph of Robert Bingham, a remote collateral ancestor. . . . He was the bishop of that see for 17 years. He was the man who passed across that very spot of ground over and over again each day.

"He was the man who knew that scene, so new to my outward experience, as he knew the palm of his own hand. But Bishop Bingham died in 1246 and was laid to his rest seven long centuries ago."[6]

How does the Bible view reincarnation? As a historian, my husband offers an interesting interpretation of the following biblical account of Jesus of Nazareth (the italics have been used for emphasis): "Shortly after His Transfiguration with Moses and Elias (Elijah), Jesus cautioned his disciples about mentioning the incident: 'Tell the vision to no man until the Son of Man be risen *again* from the dead.' Whereupon the dis-

---

5. Barry Bingham, *Louisville Courier-Journal and Times*, September 1, 1963.
6. Ibid., pp. 28, 29.

ciples stated that it was written that Elias must first *return* before the Son of God.

"And Jesus answered and said unto them, *'Elias truly shall first come, and restore all things.'*

" 'But I say unto you, *that Elias is come already, and they knew him not,* but have done unto him whatsoever they listed. Likewise shall also the Son of man suffer of them.' [Matt. 17:1–13.]

"The disciples realized Jesus was speaking of John the Baptist as the rebirth of Elias. This acceptance by Jesus of John the Baptist as the return of Elias was in keeping with Orthodox Jewish teachings that proclaimed Elias as the rebirth of Moses. Thus in both the Old and New Testaments, the idea of reincarnation was accepted. Indeed, the coming of the Messiah was the ultimate in a belief in salvation through rebirth."

We questioned Alex Tanous about this biblical concept. Although Dr. Tanous does not believe that he himself has been reincarnated, he does believe in the biblical reincarnation very strongly. "The spirit is born. The spirit is the continuing of the creativity of man as far as I am concerned. Spirit does not die. It can take on a personality and you may believe that is what you are. It can be creative or destructive. Spirit again is mind. It is knowledge. Christ said 'I must go to send you the Spirit.' "

When asked if he believed that Elias (Elijah) came back in the flesh of John the Baptist, Dr. Tanous replied: "What I want to say is the individuality of Elijah was not born again. That is the soul. Elijah the person, the individuality of Elijah, did not return." He cautioned that we should not be too fast in saying, "This is this, or this is that. We should be open to all of this. I am still open to reincarnation. I want to know what reincarnation really means. What returned when Christ said Elijah has come and gone is the spirit or the continuation of Elijah's unfinished work. The spirit was unfinished."

Dr. Tanous differentiates between the spirit and the soul: "Spirit means one thing. It does not mean soul. Soul is another word. Soul is the individuality that is you after life. The spirit is a different entity totally. Therefore, spirit must go on in its creativity—that is, the creative person in each one of us. A lot of people talk about spirit and soul being one. They are not. They are two different entities."

Why would souls reincarnate? It has been suggested that if there indeed *is* survival after death, then it would follow that the possibility for reincarnation is very strong. One theory holds that some souls can reincarnate almost immediately after death. Another theory suggests there is a "waiting period" before reincarnation can take place. In a somewhat different context, still another theory is that we reincarnate in order to benefit from "lessons" learned in the previous incarnations. Others believe it is just the way of the world to keep reincarnating, with no specific learning process involved.

Does acceptance of the theory of survival indicate acceptance of the theory of reincarnation as well? In correspondence with Dr. John Kappas of the Hypnosis Motivation Institute in California, I queried him in connection with his hypnosis of the famous actor, Glenn Ford, who, while in hypnotic trance, "regressed" to five earlier lives: a Roman in the third century; a British sailor in 1666, who died at an early age in the Great Plague of London; a guard at the Palace of French King Louis XIV in 1680; a music teacher in Scotland in 1840; and a cowboy in 1885. Asked whether, if the theory of survival after death were accepted as valid in some quarters, then the theory of previous lives could be accepted as well. Dr. Kappas replied:

"I believe that the theory of life after death in a biblical sense, and the theory of pre-birth regression or reincarnation are basically the same thing. It is a matter of semantics. In my studies of comparative religions and metaphysics my interpretation is that this concept has been present in all of the biblical writings as well as the philosophies of the past."

I recall an interesting conversation I had with the brilliant Dr. Nandor Fodor many, many years ago. I remember telling him that I wished I knew that once life was finished, as we know it, that we could know it was really the end. I told him I wanted to be cremated because I felt that might be the best way of attempting to call halt and cease to a continuous process. He laughed and explained the nature of energy to me. However, the end result was interesting, that we both became members of the same funeral society where we could have our cremation wishes accomplished.

It would be nice to know if, when making the final crossing, we could hope to reach the place Nandor Fodor described in his last words: "I am going home."

The Summing Up

There can be no summary.
It is not finished.
The mind goes on forever.

—Katherine Fair Donnelly

Glossary

Agent. The person sending a telepathic message.

Astral flight (*astral projection*). The theory of the soul departing temporarily from the physical body, especially during sleep. According to this concept, the psyche can wander freely at will, returning later to the sleeping body.

Atman. In the Hindu religion: the Universal Principle or the Divine Soul.

Aura. The halo, light, or nimbus that emanates from and surrounds every human being.

Automatic writer. A medium or sensitive who produces written messages from either a discarnate spirit or an unknown source.

Automatism. Psychic states and movements made without conscious thought or will.

Bilocation. The state of being projected into two places at one time.

Chance. The area of unexpected causal factors that are unimportant to the purpose of an event.

Clairvoyance. The perception of distant events or people without the use of the normal five senses—i.e., "seeing" a distant event simultaneously with its happening.

Cloud chamber. An experimental apparatus developed by physicists to measure the path of nuclear particles and now used to detect the energy given off by a healer or psychic.

Communication. A written or verbal message received by a medium or sensitive from an external intelligence.

Control. The "spirit" intelligence that sends messages to a medium while in trance.

Discarnate. The soul, personality, or intelligence of a person or animal who has died.

Dissociation. The splitting of the personality into two or more separate parts; thus either a dual personality (two) or a multiple personality (three or more).

Dowsing. The use of an inanimate object to detect the presence of underground water, oil, gold, or other metals.

ESP. Extrasensory perception: awareness of objects, events, or thoughts from either near or far without the use of the five normal senses.

Guide. See *control.*

Guru. In the Hindu religion: a spiritual or religious teacher.

Hallucination. A sensory perception with no objective reality in the areas of sight, hearing, smell, etc.

Healer. See *Psychic healer.*

Karma. In the Hindu religion: the universal law of cause and effect. One carries his "sins" from a previous life to the present one.

Kirlian photography. Developed by a Russian electrician in 1939. It is a process of color photography that measures the radiations emanating from living organisms—i.e., auras.

Levitation. The raising of objects or people from the ground without using any physical means. Generally accomplished by a physical medium.

Medium. A man or woman who acts as a communication between the living and the spirit world. A person who is in contact with discarnate souls.

Mental healer. See *psychic healer.*

Mental medium. A man or woman who produces messages from the spirits of the departed while in trance state.

Message. The communication received by a medium while in either a trance or a state of automatism. It is presumed that the "mesesage" comes from an intelligence outside of the medium.

Mind-and-body control. The manipulating of the involuntary functions of the body—i.e., stopping the breathing process for long periods of time.

Out-of-body experience. The traveling of the soul through space, leaving the physical body behind at rest or asleep.

Paradiagnostics. A medical diagnosis received clairvoyantly with no physical contact between doctor and patient.

Paramedicine. The same as mental healing or psychic healing. The healing by unexplained methods of illnesses that defy orthodox medicine.

Paranormal. Beyond or above normal means.

Parapsychology. The study of extrasensory perception (ESP) which lies beyond the scope of orthodox psychologists. Also the name given to psychical research.

Percipient. The person who receives telepathic or clairvoyant messages.

Physical medium. A person who produces the movement of objects on things through the intervention of discarnate spirits.

Poltergeist. From the German: A noisy ghost responsible for many mischievous events—e.g., hurling of rocks and breaking objects.

Prana. In the Hindu religion: the universal energy; the sum of everything.

Precognition. The foretelling of an event that has not yet happened—an event that the percipient had no way of knowing of in advance.

Psi. A general term used in the place of the more technical "psychic" and "parapsychical." Similar to ESP.

Psychic healer. A person who cures mental and physical illnesses through the laying on of hands; the invocation of God or a discarnate spirit to activate the healing process.

Psychokinesis (PK). The direct influence a person exerts upon an object or thing without the use of any physical energy. The moving of an object through mental power alone. Better known as "mind over matter."

Retrocognition. Knowledge of past events received paranormally. "Seeing" the past without any knowledge of it.

Séance. The meeting of several people with a medium for the object of receiving messages from discarnate souls.

Sensitive. The contemporary title given to a medium. A medium who does not necessarily go into a trance to receive messages.

Shanti. In the Hindu religion: the divine peace; the Universal Place. Also a benediction.

Spiritualist. A person who believes in life after death and in his or her ability to contact departed souls either directly or through a medium.

Subject. A person who is experimented upon in ESP tests. Generally, the percipient (receiver) in such tests.

Subliminal. Ideas, thoughts, or sights lying beneath the surface of ordinary consciousness.

Telekinesis. The movement of objects or things without the use of existing physical force. An older term similar to "psychokinesis."

Telepathy. The sending of mental messages of any kind from one person to another without the apparent use of the normal senses.

Thought transference. The awareness of another person's thoughts at the moment the subject is thinking of them. This process is generally called "telepathy."

Yama. In the Hindu religion: the ethical teaching necessary for union or self-realization.

Selected Bibliography

Aldiss, B. W. *The Shape of Further Things*. Garden City, N.Y.: Doubleday & Co., 1970.

Ashby, R. H. *The Guide Book for the Study of Psychical Research*. New York, Samuel Weiser, 1972.

Balakian, Anna. *André Breton*. New York: Oxford University Press, 1971.

Barbanell, M. *This Is Spiritualism*. London: Herbert Jenkins, 1959.

Bardens, Dennis. *Ghosts and Hauntings*. New York: Taplinger Publishing Co., 1968.

Bayless, R. *The Enigma of the Poltergeist*. New York: Parker Publishing Co., 1967.

Beard, Paul. *Survival of Death*. London: Hodder and Stoughton, 1966.

Carr, D. E. *The Eternal Return*. Garden City, N.Y.: Doubleday & Co., 1968.

Carrington, H. *The Physical Phenomena of Spiritualism*. New York: Herbert Turner & Co., 1907.

Cerminara, Gina. *Many Mansions*. New York: New American Library, Signet Book, 1967.

Cerutti, Edwina. *Olga Worrall: Mystic with the Healing Hands*. New York: Harper & Row, 1975.

Cohen, Daniel. *ESP—The Search Beyond the Senses*. New York: Harcourt Brace Jovanovich, 1973.

Crookes, W. *Researches in the Phenomena of Spiritualism*. London: J. Burns, 1874.

Cummins, G. *Swan on a Black Sea: A Study in Automatic Writing*. New York: Samuel Weiser, 1970.

Curtis, R. H. *On ESP*. Englewood Cliffs, N.J.: Prentice-Hall, 1974.

Dingwall, C. J. *Some Human Oddities*. New York: University Books, 1962.

Edwards, Harry. *The Power of Healing*. London: Tandem Books, 1968.

Flammarion, Camille. *The Unknown*. New York: Harper & Brothers, 1900.

Flammonde, Paris. *The Mystic Healers*. New York: Stein and Day, 1974.

Fodor, Nandor. *On the Trail of the Poltergeist*. New York: The Citadel Press, 1958.

Galloway, Donald. *Inevitable Journey*. London: Frederick Mullter, 1974.

Garrett, Eileen J. *Adventures in the Supernormal*. New York: Paperback Library, Inc., 1968.

————. *Beyond the Five Senses.* New York: J. B. Lippincott Co., 1957.

————. *Life Is the Healer.* Philadelphia: Dorrance & Co., 1957.

————. *Many Voices.* New York: G. P. Putnam's Sons, 1968.

————. *Telepathy.* New York: Helix Press, 1968.

Greenhouse, Herbert. *The Book of Psychic Knowledge.* New York: Taplinger Publishing Co., 1973.

Hammond, David. *The Search for Psychic Power.* New York: Bantam Books, 1975.

Hansel, C. E. M. *ESP: A Scientific Evaluation,* New York: Charles Scribner's Sons, 1966.

Heywood, Rosalind. *The Sixth Sense.* London: Chatto & Windus, 1959.

Hintze, Naomi A., and Pratt, J. Gaither. *The Psychic Realm: What Can You Believe?.* New York: Random House, Inc., 1975.

Holms, Campbell. *The Facts of Psychic Science and Philosophy.* London: Kegan, Paul, Trench, Trubner, 1925.

Holzer, Hans. *ESP and You.* New York: Hawthorne Books, 1972.

Johnson, R. C. *The Imprisoned Splendour.* New York, Harper & Brothers, 1953.

————. *Psychical Research.* New York: Philosophical Library, 1956.

Jung, C. G. *The Structure and Dynamics of the Psyche.* New York: Pantheon, 1960.

LeShan, Lawrence. *The Medium, the Mystic and the Physicist.* New York: Viking Press, 1966.

————. *How to Meditate.* Boston, Little, Brown & Co., 1974.

Litkei, A. F. *ESP: An Account of the Fabulous in Our Everyday Life.* New York: Hanlit Publications, 1967.

Lodge, Oliver. *The Survival of Man.* New York: G. H. Doran & Co., 1909.

Osborn, A. W. *The Expansion of Awareness.* Surrey: The Omega Press, 1955.

————. *The Meaning of Personal Existence.* Illinois: The Theosophical Publishing House, 1966.

Ostrander, S., and Shroeder, L. *Handbook of Psychic Discoveries.* New York: Berkley Pub., 1974.

————. *Psychic Discoveries Behind the Iron Curtain.* Englewood Cliffs, N.J.: Prentice-Hall, Inc., 1970.

Osty, Eugene. *Supernormal Faculties in Man.* London: Methuen, 1923.

Prince, W. F. *The Case of Patience Worth.* Boston: The Boston Society for Psychic Research, 1924.

Roberts, Estelle. *Fifty Years a Medium.* New York: Avon Books, 1959.

Rogo, D. Scott. *Parapsychology: A Century Of Inquiry.* New York: Dell Publishing Co., 1975.

Roll, W. G. *The Poltergeist.* New York: Nelson Doubleday, 1972.

Staff, Vera S. *Remembered on Waking.* Sussex, England: Churches Fellowship for Psychical and Spiritual Studies, 1975.

Stearn, Jess. *The Door to the Future.* Garden City, N.Y.: Doubleday & Co., 1963.

Tanous, Alex, with Ardman, H. *Beyond Coincidence.* Garden City, N.Y., Doubleday, 1976.

Wilson, Colin. *The Occult: A History*. New York: Random House, Inc., 1971.

Worrall, Ambrose and Olga. *The Miracle Healers*. New York: Harper & Row, 1965.

Wright, Theon. *The Open Door*. New York: The John Day Co., 1970.

Xavier, F. C., and Vieira, W. *The World of the Spirit*. New York: Philosophical Library, 1966.

Additional Reading Suggestions

by Ruby Yeatman

Bach, Richard. *Johnathan Livingston Seagull.* 1970.
Baird, A. T. *One Hundred Cases for Survival.* 1943.
Barrett, Sir William. *Death Bed Visions.* 1926.
Cummins, Geraldine. *Beyond Human Personality.* 1935.
————. *The Road to Immortality.* 1932.
————. *Travellers in Eternity.* 1948.
Greaves, Helen. *The Dissolving Veil.* 1967.
————. *The Wheel of Eternity.* 1974.
Greber, Johannes. *Communication with the Spirit World.* New York, 1932.
Heywood, Rosalind. *The Infinite Hive.* 1964.
Jacobson, Nils. *Life Without Death?* 1974. Psychical research.
Karagulla, Dr. Shafika. *Breakthrough to Creativity.* 1967.
Kennedy, the Rev. David. *Venture in Immortality.* 1973.
Lehmann, Rosamond. *Swan in the Evening.* 1967.
Lodge, Sir Oliver. *Evolution and Creation.* 1926.
Pauchard, Albert. *The Other World.* 1973. Reprint.
Payne, Phoebe, and Bendit, Laurence. *The Psychic Sense.* 1943.
Randall, John L. *Parapsychology and the Nature of Life.* 1975. Psychical
    research.
Rauscher, the Rev. William. *The Spiritual Frontier: A Priest Explores the
    Psychic World.* New York, 1975.
Shepherd, Dr. A. P. *The Eternity of Time.* 1941.
Sherwood, Jane. *The Country Beyond.* 1945. Reprint.
Trinder, W. H. *Dowsing.* 1939.
Vitae, Quaestor. *The Process of Man's Becoming.*
Warrick, F. W. *Experiments in Psychics.* 1946.
Weatherhead, the Rev. Leslie. *Life Begins at Death.* 1969.
White, Stewart E. *The Betty Book.* 1937.
Whymant, Dr. Neville. *Psychic Adventures in New York.* 1931.

NOTE: For information on where to obtain books not easily accessible, see
    Appendix.

Note to the Reader

Some of the books suggested for additional reading may not be obtainable in libraries in your area. An excellent source for locating psychic books is Samuel Weiser, Inc., which supplies information about books on a variety of psychic subjects. For a nominal charge, you may obtain the Weiser catalogue by writing to them at 734 Broadway, New York, New York 10003. Another good source for top-line information on books and research in the psychic field is Scarecrow Press, Inc., 52 Liberty Street, P.O. Box 656, Metuchen, New Jersey 08840. Many times an older psychic book has been put out in paperback. For example, *The Betty Book*, by Stewart E. White, published in 1937, was published in paperback by E. P. Dutton Co. in 1977. For another source in locating psychic books there is the YES Bookshop, 1035 31 Street, N.W., Washington, D.C. 20007. Also available is a comprehensive guide on many subjects in print, including psychic books, entitled "The Yes Guide."

Appendix: Addresses for Psychic Information

INFORMATION ON PSYCHIC GROUPS

The American Society for Psychical Research, 5 West 73 Street, New York, New York 10023. Prestigious pioneer group provides a great deal of basic information to scientists and the public alike on psychic matters. Provides members with a number of highly regarded psi publications including the *ASPR Newsletter* and the *Journal*, as well as housing an excellent psi library. You may obtain a 16-page directory, *Courses and Other Opportunities in Parapsychology*, which provides information about lectures and instruction at universities within your proximity. Inquiries about membership or other information should be sent to the above address with a stamped, self-addressed envelope.

The Association for Research and Enlightenment, P.O. Box 595, Virginia Beach, Virginia 23451. This is a national association and can refer you to local chapters. Has extensive readings and works of Cayce in their library.

ESP Research Associates Foundation, Union National Plaza, Suite 1630, Little Rock, Arkansas 72201. The workshop of this group, with Harold Sherman as its director, is well known in psychic circles.

Foundation for Research on the Nature of Man, 402 Buchanan, Durham, North Carolina 27708. This highly regarded foundation publishes the *Journal of Parapsychology*, and its director is the famous pioneer Dr. Joseph B. Rhine of the Institute of Parapsychology in Durham.

Parapsychology Foundation, 29 West 57 Street, New York, New York. Has one of the most complete psi libraries in the country, which is open to the public. Publishes proceedings of annual conferences as well as a Parapsychological Monograph series. Also available at a nominal charge is the *Parapsychology Review*, a comprehensive newsletter with latest developments in worldwide events, articles, and research reports.

Psychical Research Foundation, Duke Station, Durham, North Carolina 27706. With the distinguished William G. Roll as director, the foundation publishes *Theta*, well regarded in the psychic field and primarily a journal for research on the question of survival after death.

The College of Psychic Studies, 16 Queensberry Place, London, England SW7 2EB. Founded in 1884 to further inquiry into psychical and allied fields. Has library of over 10,000 volumes. Weekly lectures are held through most of year, as well as weekend workshops, classes for meditation, and many brief lecture courses given by distinguished personalities in the psychic field. Under the guidance of Paul Beard, president, the College sponsors a quarterly journal, entitled *Light*, which contains articles by well-known writers on aspects of psychical research, evidence for survival of bodily death, and the inner nature of man.

The Spiritual Frontiers Fellowship, Executive Plaza, 10715 Winner Road, Independence, Missouri 64052. This is a national organization whose *Journal* is published by a nondenominational group of clergy and laypeople who are exploring psychic phenomena, healing, and mystical experiences. There are local chapters located throughout the United States.

SPECIAL NOTE

Because of the increasing number of parapsychological associations, there are too many to list in this small space. However, names of additional psychic groups may many times be found in psychic publications. For example, one such listing may be obtained from the Parapsychology Foundation (address shown above). In vol. 6, no. 1 (the January-February 1975 issue) of their Newsletter, the *Parapsychology Review*, there is a listing entitled "Directory of Parapsychological Associations." As well, a selected listing of parapsychology periodicals appears in the May-June 1977 issue, vol. 8, no. 3. Details on other psychic groups and new publications, as well as courses, lectures, and other happenings in different parts of the country, appear many times in announcement sections of various publications, some of which are listed below.

INFORMATION ON PSYCHIC MAGAZINES, JOURNALS, AND NEWSLETTERS

Brain Mind Bulletin, published twice monthly by Interface Press, P.O. Box 42211, Los Angeles, California 90042. This highly regarded newsletter covers research discoveries, new theories, news of conferences and workshops, latest books and journals, government policies, and new developments.

Psychic News, with over 100,000 readers, has weekly newspaper-type coverage of spiritualistic and psychic news as well as book reviews. Write air mail to: 23 Great Queen Street, London WC2B-5BB, England.

New Realities (formerly *Psychic Magazine*), P.O. Box 26289, Custom House, San Francisco, California 94126. Covers holistic health, consciousness, various aspects of parapsychology, modern mysticism, life styles, as well as news and articles for the layperson. Interviews with leading personalities in the psychic world.

The Parapsychology Review, 29 West 57 Street, New York, New York.

10019. The Parapsychology Foundation's newsletter covers newest developments in the psychic field as well as worldwide news. Published bimonthly.

Journal of the American Society for Psychical Research, 5 West 73 Street, New York, New York 10023. Considered one of the major journals in parapsychology, with articles on various aspects of parapsychology, research reports, correspondence, book reviews, notices, and news in the psychic field.

ASPR Newsletter, 5 West 73 Street, New York, New York 10023. A comprehensive digest of latest developments in parapsychology, news of psychic events, as well as educational directions in the field, reviews of books, and announcements. Reports are written by top professionals in "lay language" in a collation of 27 key articles from the *Newsletter*, entitled "Exploring ESP and PK," and will be most useful to students, teachers, discussion leaders, and interested laypeople who want to know of current developments in the psychic field.

Journal of the British Society for Psychical Research, 1 Adam & Eve Mews, London W8 England. Published quarterly by the oldest psychical research society, begun in 1882. The *Journal* includes various scientific reports, articles, spontaneous cases, book reviews, news, and notices.

Psychology Today, Reader Service, P.O. Box 700, Del Mar, California 92014. In addition to various articles on psi-related topics, has listing of tapes offered on psychic phenomena.

Light, quarterly journal of The College of Psychic Studies, 16 Queensberry Place, London SW7 2EB, England. With a worldwide circulation, it contains articles by well-known writers on evidence for survival of bodily death, the inner nature of man, and various aspects of psychical research.

Fate, a forerunner of magazines popularizing the psychic field, including stories, articles, psychic news, the publisher's column, and books column. Published by Clark Publishing Co., 500 Hyacinth Place, Highland Park, Illinois 60035.

Journal of Parapsychology, published by Parapsychology Press, Box 6847, College Station, Durham, North Carolina 27708. One of the pioneer scientific journals, covering ESP, psychokinesis, and associated subjects.

Theta, the journal of the Psychical Research Foundation, primarily deals with research on survival after death. Published four times a year. Duke Station, Durham, North Carolina 27706.

INFORMATION ON BOOKS

An excellent source for psychic books is Samuel Weiser, Inc., which supplies information about books on a variety of psychic subjects. For a nominal charge, you may obtain the Weiser catalogue by writing to them at 734 Broadway, New York, New York 10003.

Another good source for top-line information on books and research in the psychic field is Scarecrow Press, Inc., 52 Liberty Street, P.O. Box 656, Metuchen, New Jersey 08840.

For locating books difficult to find, a helpful source is the YES Bookshop, 1035 31 Street, N.W., Washington, D.C. 20007.

If you are looking for a specific book and cannot locate it, write to the publisher.

INFORMATION ON TAPES

Talks by many well-known persons on psychic matters are available from many sources, some of which are:

The Association for Research and Enlightenment, c/o A.R.E. Tape Library, 2326 East Aldine, Phoenix, Arizona 85022, offers a tape catalogue in connection with the Edgar Cayce work, as well as meditation and other psychic areas.

Science of Mind Symposium, P.O. Box 75127, Los Angeles, California 90075, has many tapes on healing by renowned individuals such as Gloria Swanson, Olga Worrall, Dr. O. Carl Simonton, etc. There is a charge of a few dollars.

Psychology Today, Reader Service, P.O. Box 700, Del Mar, California 92014, provides a current list of available tapes.

INDEX

Index